Real Life Adventure

Fused with Spiritual Adrenaline!

Tristin,
God loves you!
Follow Him and
Commit w/ PASSION!

Mike Tison

Rom 10:9-10

Copyright © 2011 Mike Tison

Published by:
Rochester Media, Inc.
PO Box 80002
Rochester, MI 48308
248-429-READ (7323)
248-430-8799 fax
info@rochestermedia.com
www.rochestermedia.com

All rights reserved. No part of this book may be reproduced or transmitted in any form or by any means including, but not limited to, electronic or mechanical, photocopying, recording, or by any information storage and retrieval system without written permission from the publisher, except for the inclusion of brief quotations in review.

Scripture quotations marked (ESV) are from The Holy Bible, English Standard Version, copyright © 2001 by Crossway Bibles, a division of Good News Publishers. Used by permission. All rights reserved.

Cover Design: Mike Tison
Cover Concept: Paul Dziepak
Cover Photo: Anja Hild

First U.S. Edition Year 1st Edition was Published

Publisher's Cataloging-In-Publication Data

Tison, Mike

Seize The Adventure
Summary: Christian devotional based on real life adventure stories.

13 Digit ISBN 978-1463518288

1. Christian Living, Spiritual Growth, Adventure, Christianity, and Religion

For current information about releases by Mike Tison or
or other releases from Rochester Media, Inc., visit our web sites:
http://www.SeizeTheAdventure.com or http://www.rochestermedia.com

Printed in the United States of America

DEDICATION

This book is dedicated to my wife, Sarah, for all of her sacrifice and love and to my mother, Marianne, who both loved me very much, but also slapped the back of my head when I needed it most. She encouraged me in everything that I did, even when it didn't make sense to anyone else.

"A strong devotional offering sure to engage and satisfy men in a field that often offers little for them."

– Bestselling author Sandra Byrd, www.sandrabyrd.com

"Mike Tison exudes a love of God's creation that motivates men to 'get out there' and learn more about the Creator. His heartfelt testimony will move you to tears – and kick you in the pants with the kind of encouragement that makes you want to get busy."

– Chuck Holton – CBN Adventure Correspondent and author

"Mike Tison has proven himself in life and conduct to be an example to others."

– Bill Bronkema – Retired Pastor, Ortonville Baptist Church

"I know that God has already and continues to use you to stretch and challenge people in their faith. Thanks for being bold."

– Ken Tison – Pastor, Hillside Bible Church

CONTENTS

DEDICATION

ENDORSEMENTS

INTRODUCTION   1

Day 1:	UNDER ATTACK - PART 1	9
Day 2:	UNDER ATTACK - PART 2	11
Day 3:	DOUBLE HYDRAULIC	13
Day 4:	SLEEPING BAG	15
Day 5:	TROUBLE IN THE CANYON – PART 1	17
Day 6:	TROUBLE IN THE CANYON – PART 2	19
Day 7:	TROUBLE IN THE CANYON – PART 3	21
Day 8:	SUNKEN TREASURE	23
Day 9:	LOST IN THE MOUNTAINS – PART 1	25
Day 10:	LOST IN THE MOUNTAINS – PART 2	27
Day 11:	LOST IN THE MOUNTAINS – PART 3	29
Day 12:	LOST IN THE MOUNTAINS – PART 4	31
Day 13:	LOST IN THE MOUNTAINS – PART 5	33
Day 14:	LOST IN THE MOUNTAINS – PART 6	35

Day 15:	LOST IN THE MOUNTAINS – PART 7	37
Day 16:	TANGLED BIRD	39
Day 17:	MOUNTAIN BIKE MUD BATH	41
Day 18:	WIDE OF THE MARK – PART 1	43
Day 19:	WIDE OF THE MARK – PART 2	45
Day 20:	WIDE OF THE MARK – PART 3	47
Day 21:	MONSTER MISS	49
Day 22:	A NIGHT HIKE	51
Day 23:	AFRAID OF GETTING HIT	53
Day 24:	A LEAP OF FAITH	55
Day 25:	LURE PIERCING	57
Day 26:	SHOOTING FRENZY	59
Day 27:	STUCK UNDERWATER – PART 1	61
Day 28:	STUCK UNDERWATER – PART 2	63
Day 29:	SITTING THE BENCH	65
Day 30:	SUPERNATURAL DESIGNER	67
Day 31:	A MAN OF FAITH	69
Day 32:	A DIVINE SOTER	71
Day 33:	FLASH FLOOD	73

Day 34:	LUCKY SHOT	75
Day 35:	LUNCH TIME STALK	77
Day 36:	MONSOON SEASON	79
	ADVENTURE NOTES – PRAYER JOURNAL	82
Day 37:	NO RECORD	83
Day 38:	DOWNHILL CRASH	85
Day 39:	LEAVING THE TRAIL EARLY	87
Day 40:	THE RECRUIT	89
Day 41:	THROUGH THE DARKNESS – PART 1	91
	ADVENTURE NOTES – PRAYER JOURNAL	94
Day 42:	THROUGH THE DARKNESS – PART 2	95
Day 43:	THROUGH THE DARKNESS – PART 3	97
Day 44:	A CRAZY DAY	99
Day 45:	A FEAR OF GOD	101
Day 46:	IMPROPER BALANCE	103
Day 47:	STORM ON THE WATER	105
Day 48:	NOT WHAT IT APPEARS	107
Day 49:	WHY A NERD WOULD HIKE – J. FOSTER	109
Day 50:	NOT ALWAYS GO BIG OR GO HOME	111

Day 51:	GRACE LIKE RAIN	113
Day 52:	UNDERCURRENT WARNING	115
Day 53:	SCOPE ADJUSTMENT	117
Day 54:	A REJECTED PLAYER	119
Day 55:	GET OUT OF THE FOG	121
Day 56:	ALL OF THE TOYS	123
Day 57:	A SPECIAL REVERENCE AND AWE	125
Day 58:	CRAZY CREATION	127
Day 59:	FAN THE FLAME	129
Day 60:	GOING HOME	131
	FAITH CHALLENGE ADVENTURE	133
	ABOUT THE AUTHOR	135
	ACKNOWLEDGMENTS	136
	ADVENTURE NOTES	137
	PRAYER JOURNAL	141

Commit with Passion!

The adventure began with two young boys running for their lives down a giant washed out hill. At the bottom lay a large, secluded lake surrounded by swamp and woods. The brothers worked their way through the tall grass, guns in hand, hoping to elude their pursuers. They stumbled upon a slowly rotting wooden row boat, hidden in the deep grass next to the water's edge. Once they realized their predicament the choice was obvious. Stay and fight and risk death, or take the boat and escape across the lake to live another day.

The boat was lodged in the mud and held captive by the roots of the weeds that surrounded it. After some effort on the boys' part, it began to move. Water splashed over the bow as it temporarily submerged and then popped back up again, as the rest of the boat floated on the surface. There were no paddles, but they did have the butt end of their guns to paddle to safety. As they worked their way across the water the old boat began to fill with water. There was still another hundred yards to go, could they make it?

Would they make it before the boat sank? Doubt began to creep in but they had no choice now. They had come too far. It was all or nothing, so they paddled faster and harder, putting all they had into their effort.

The summer sun beat down on the two escapees and sweat dripped from their foreheads. Their clammy hands made it difficult to hang on-to the metal gun barrels. The youngest, riding in the front, lost his grip and watched as his gun slipped out of his hands, quickly and silently sinking to the bottom. He wondered if resting at the bottom of this dark and deep lake was going to be their fate as well. That gun had saved his life numerous times, but now his survival and his hope to reach the shore safely rested on the strength of his brother. The water continued to rise.

The bow of the boat crashed into the swampy shoreline. They jumped out of the boat and sank deep in the mud. It was a struggle to get to firm ground, but they were just happy to make it to safety, knowing they hadn't drowned in a sinking death trap. The boys looked at the boat and then across the shore and then looked at their mud-soaked clothes and laughed.

"Let's get some lunch!" the oldest commanded.

"Do you think Dad will be mad I lost my BB gun?"

"I don't know, but it was definitely worth the adventure."

When I was a child my imagination and my ambition for adventure always contained elements of risk, challenges, thrills, or conquests. Whether it was playing make believe soldiers, riding motorcycles with reckless abandon, playing war with firecrackers, or playing for hours in the woods; adventure was always at the forefront of our minds. It was great having an older brother who helped foster this natural built-in desire. However, as I have grown into an adult, my ambitions changed and matured. My brother is still there helping me, but instead of engaging in childhood adventures we are both committed to living out our faith with the same adventure-style we had when we were kids growing up in the countryside.

God wired man from the very beginning to seek after adventure. It is evident in toddlers, young boys, young men, and adults. For example: men and boys like to hunt and fish, participate in outdoor activities, hike, kayak, play sports, drive fast cars, race motorcycles, fly in planes, pursue a woman, and make more money so they can engage in more adventure. It is normal for men to seek adventure.

After all, God designed us in his own image, which means that God too has an adventurous side. God chooses to seek after you, and in return he wants you to seek after him. God is amazing and beyond our wildest dreams. Discovering Him and developing a deeper relationship with Him is the best adventure that you could ever possibly engage in. A friend once told me that when we get to heaven, "Heaven won't be boring. Every day is going to be a new day of discovering something new about God – a life of eternal discovery."

Outside of man lies a world of bold undertakings and exciting experiences, but true adventure takes place inside. Adventure lies within all of us, but who we become on the outside is just an echo emanating from our inner being. It all begins in the heart and flows out from there. Our life focus needs to have an eternal perspective, otherwise we just start to imitate the world and begin an aimless wandering. Our heart determines our direction. What we allow to fill our hearts and minds will determine who we become.

My purpose is to motivate, inspire, encourage and strengthen you to live your life for Jesus Christ. It is my goal to challenge you to jumpstart your faith and to seek after God in a way that brings your faith to life again. Just like when you were a child, by having a love of the pursuit, a reckless faith, a trusting heart and a lasting hope that no matter the challenge the outcome will always be worth the adventure. It is my hope that you will take this opportunity to commit with passion and to seize your adventure the way God intended.

Each day brings a new challenge. In order to help you engage, understand, apply, and commit with passion these specific elements will help:

1. **Key Verse** – English Standard Version (ESV). Scripture is God's Word. Reflecting or memorizing these verses will help you draw into a more personal and intimate relationship with Him. It is important to be able to recall scripture in order to resist temptation, to use for comfort, to receive encouragement, and to learn more about God or gain guidance and direction for your life.

2. **True Story** – Personal stories of adventure that draw spiritual parallels and reinforce the main theme.

3. **Key Quote** – Quips from Christian authors, preachers and those who have gone before us seizing the adventure God had for them. These are meant to inspire and to cause you to think about the spiritual topic.

4. **Key Question or Statement** – Meant to help you reflect on the lesson and to examine your own heart.

5. **Response Item** – Activities designed to engage you in a more intimate relationship with God.

   - Prayer – spend time in prayer communicating with God.
   - Bible readings – Read the assigned readings to gain further insight on the topic.
   - Meditation – Take time to reflect on the statement or question.
   - Solitude – Go and find a place of solitude to spend time with just you and God.
   - Self-examination – Ask God to search out your heart. Be open and honest.
   - Faith Challenge – Engage in the assigned activity at the end of the book to awaken your faith.

- Fast – Participate in a one or three day liquid fast. No food, just water or juice.
- Lists – Things you write down based on what is asked of you. Write in the book.

6. **Adventure Notes** – This is an area in the back of the book to write down your ideas and thoughts or whatever else comes to your mind. It is free space for you to use as you wish. Don't be afraid to write in this book and mess it up with notes and thoughts.

7. **Prayer Journal** - Write down prayer requests in the back pages as you think of them. When a prayer request is answered, place a check mark in the **Yes**, **No**, or **Grow** box.

    - **Yes** – God answered your prayer request in the way that you had hoped.
    - **No** – God answered your prayer request with an outcome different from what you had hoped. Remember God is sovereign and He knows best.
    - **Grow** – This may be a prayer request that requires continual growth or that God has chosen to delay his answer for some reason.

Read this book straight through or read it one day at a time. It is your call. It is your adventure. But, know that it is my prayer that each story engages you and that the material that follows resonates in your heart and mind, fanning your faith into a raging flame that compels you toward great things for God, but most importantly that helps you commit your heart to seeking after Jesus Christ.

MIKE TISON

"Be sober minded; be watchful. Your adversary the devil prowls around like a roaring lion, seeking someone to devour. Resist him..."
I Peter 5:8-9 (ESV)

UNDER ATTACK – PART 1

It was a cold, dark, and dreary day. The sky looked as though it wanted to snow again, but it held back for some unknown reason. Not that it mattered, because today was already turning out to be one of the hardest and worst days of Gene's life. Would he have enough endurance? Would he have the will to do whatever it took? The pains from his injuries increased with every step. The steep mountain terrain, combined with the mossy, dark timber, made navigation difficult. In order to make it out alive, he would have to find the way through nearly two miles of rough landscape. On three different occasions, he lay down in the snow and prayed that the Lord would take him home. On this day, God had a different plan for this sixty-eight year old hunter.

Gene Moe was in the process of field dressing a Sitka black tail deer on Raspberry Island, Alaska, when a seven hundred-fifty pound Kodiak bear approached the perimeter without notice. The distracted hunter busily focused on the task at hand. He was unaware of the lurking danger until a blood-curdling roar bellowed from the bear, shaking the woods. Surprised, Gene wheeled around with a heart and liver in one hand and a three and three quarter inch folding

Buck knife in the other. A battle of epic proportions would soon take place pitting man against beast. To be continued...

> "The devil is nimble; he can run apace; he is light of foot; he hath overtaken many....They that would have heaven must run for it."
>
> — John Bunyan

Danger is always lurking. In order to be prepared for a possible attack or to resist temptation we must pray and read the Bible. When Jesus was tempted by the evil one in the wilderness he used Scripture to put down Satan's temptations. Resisting temptation is a bold undertaking. That is why it is extremely important that we are prepared for whatever is thrown our way. We should surround our families in prayer and study the Word of God so that Scripture can be our weapon against temptation. It never hurts to find other men who seek after God to help hold you accountable.

What safeguards have you set up to protect you from sin?

Read 1 Peter 5 and spend time in prayer asking God for spiritual protection.

"Beloved, do not be surprised at the fiery trial when it comes upon you to test you, as though something strange were happening to you."
I Peter 4:12 (ESV)

UNDER ATTACK – PART 2

The bear, quick to strike, grasped Gene Moe firmly in his grip. The giant Kodiak bit into Gene's right arm, just above the elbow, and didn't let go. Gene fought back as best as he could and began to hit and jab his fingers into the bear's ear. This was enough to loosen the bear's clenched teeth and Gene was able to pull his arm free. A wrestling match ensued and the old hunter found out the hard way that he was in the wrong weight class. The bear easily drove him to the ground.

The hungry sow rose up on her hind legs, circling her prey, waiting to deliver the knock-out punch. Familiar with bear behavior, Gene was ready for the swipe of her claw. The bear missed, but not without slicing his earlobe in the process. Immediately, the bear dropped to all fours and knocked Gene flat on his back. Using his boots he kicked up as hard as he could into the bear's chest. The bear rolled and Gene sprung to his feet. The bear managed to bite into his right leg, just above the knee. Fighting through the intense pain, Gene was able to wrap his arms around the head of the beast and began stabbing and slicing into the bear's neck and vertebrae with his hunting knife. Surprised by this sudden attack, the blood-covered bear moved outside the battle arena.

It seems the Kodiak was determined to beat down the wounded man; she took one last charge, hoping, it would seem, to finish off her prey. "Help me, Lord!" Gene cried, and was immediately armed with new boldness. He took on the bear and stood his ground. He did not retreat, but smacked the angry sow square in the nose with his left fist forcing the bear to the ground. She never flinched when he put two bullets into his adversary.

"Many of us suffer from temptations from which we have no business to suffer."
– Oswald Chambers

Only by the grace, and strength, of God did Gene Moe make it down the mountain. He required massive amounts of treatment and surgery to put his body back together. If you are faced with a fiery trial of some kind, how will you handle it? Will you call out to God for help or try to lone wolf it – to your harm?

Second Chance: Have you set up spiritual safe guards?

Read 1 Peter 4:12-19 and take a few minutes to list out ways to safeguard your spiritual walk.

"Therefore, preparing your minds for action, and being sober-minded, set your hope fully on the grace that will be brought to you at the revelation of Jesus Christ"
1 Peter 1:13 (ESV)

DOUBLE HYDRAULIC

The buoyancy of the life jacket lifted me to the violent surface; I gasped for air and then quickly disappeared underwater again. I was in a fight, struggling to get my head above water, but I was losing. The raging river was winning. It had a hold on me and it surely wasn't about to let go. I surfaced again, and quickly inhaled a mixture of air and cold water, instantly setting my lungs on fire. This cycle continued over and over again, until the first hydraulic finally released my cold and battered body.

For the moment, the river had set me free. I had entered a dangerous part of the river without showing it proper respect. I'd entered the Double Hydraulic rapid backwards, unprepared, and preoccupied by a conversation with a nearby raft. The roar of the rapids alerted me to the coming danger, but by then it was already too late. A hydraulic or a hole is a whitewater rapid where water flows over a submerged object resulting in the water to flow back upstream creating a recirculating process. These can be very dangerous, because the rapid chooses when to spit out any object caught in its wash-cycle.

Quickly adjusting my body in the water I assumed a proper float position, with my feet facing down river, hoping to make it through the second hydraulic spin-cycle experience. This hydraulic presented a gentle slide down into a waiting six foot wall of turbulent water. I braced for impact just before my helpless body slammed into the monster wall. The rapid had its way with me and I would not see the surface again for some time.

"Having hit a wall, the next logical step is not to bang our heads against it."
– S. Harper

Often we ignore the warning signs and enter into sin caught off guard, but forced to pay the consequences of our actions. And many times it is a turbulent struggle to get out of our sin and then we expect God to sort out our mess with little or no consequence. On the river there are rules to abide by for your safety and enjoyment. They are not put into place to dampen your experience, but to keep you safe and to give you freedom to enjoy the ride without fear of disaster. God's boundaries are meant to do the same thing.

Are you caught up in a wash-cycle of sin?

Read 1 Peter 1 and take a few minutes to pray and confess your sins to God and get out of the sin-cycle.

SEIZE THE ADVENTURE – Commit with Passion

"Great is the Lord, and greatly to be praised, and his greatness is unsearchable."
Psalm 145:3 (ESV)

SLEEPING BAG

The chilly morning air froze my nose. A frosty cloud percolated from my mouth with every breath. The air temperature overnight had dropped into the low thirties and most of the men in our hiking troop were not prepared for a frozen wonderland when they signed up for a late summer excursion.

It was 6:00 am, on the North Rim of the Grand Canyon. Time to get up and descend into the great abyss for an unbelievable adventure, but the heat of the sleeping bag would not release me from its grip, and I did not resist. After a few minutes of soaking up the warmth, my thoughts drifted towards the sights and sounds that this day would bring. Restless, I attempted to unzip and free myself from my captor, but its spell was powerful. It would be a struggle.

The emotional security of staying in my current surroundings was intoxicating and extremely difficult to let go, but the risk-reward quotient of hiking the Grand Canyon outweighed any desire to stay in a place of comfort and miss out on a great adventure.

"God loves you just the way you are, but he refuses to leave you that way."
— Max Lucado

Like the sleeping bag our Christian culture is often complicit in creating a cocooned lifestyle that provides a warm feeling, but doesn't allow us to stretch our spiritual legs. We get so comfortable in our current surroundings that we lose sight of what lies on the outside of the closed zipper. Adventure is out there!

God has called each of us to an adventure, to a life of worship and service. He wants to stretch you and to move you into a position that leads you to lean on Him. Don't give in to the comfort of normal; it only leads to spiritual complacency.

Is your faith like being inside of a cocoon?

Read Psalm 145, pray and ask God to show you how to think big when it comes to faith. After all, He is a diverse God and his greatness is unsearchable.

"My son, keep your father's commandment, and forsake not your mother's teaching. Bind them on your heart always; tie them around your neck."
Proverbs 6:20-21 (ESV)

TROUBLE IN THE CANYON – PART 1

There was a chill in the air, it was morning and all signs pointed towards it growing into a beautiful day. The long descent into the Grand Canyon would be both beautiful and challenging. The men were excited to get going and ready to complete the rim to rim hike.

As the day drew on their boots became covered in orange trail dust and their bodies dripped with sweat. With each step, and every switchback, the men's playful banter diminished till the lead hiker woke them with a yell, "SNAKE!" Somebody in the group screamed. The hikers froze and then carefully maneuvered safely around the large Arizona rattlesnake. Done sunbathing, the snake slithered up the trail and into a hole in the side of the canyon wall. Laughing and poking fun, the men continued.

"Man! You screamed like a girl seeing a spider for the first time." One of the men quipped.

"No, I didn't!" the culprit defended himself. "Yes, you did." The group said in unison.

In life, every once in a while an opportunity like no other presents itself, begging to see that it doesn't get wasted. For me it was the chance to take the lead position. Moments later, I spotted a stick the same color, shape and size of the rattlesnake we had just seen. Seizing the opportunity, I propelled the fake snake backward into the group of hikers with my trekking pole, hollering, "SNAKE!" The stick bounced off of the legs of the first two hikers directly behind me and came to rest at the feet of the third hiker. It's too bad that there wasn't any video of all of the dancing, sights and sounds that this practical joke created. And for the record, more than one man screamed in a high-pitched voice.

"Do not be deceived; happiness and enjoyment do not lie in wicked ways."
— Isaac Watts

The reason this joke worked so well was that it was put into motion twenty minutes after the real snake had presented itself. Enough time had passed that the men had let their guard down, but the real danger was still present, lingering in the back of their minds. Danger is everywhere, especially when you have committed to a life of serving God. Be alert and be prepared, as you live out your faith, to discern which dangers are real, and which only seem to be.

The evil one is subtle.
be alert and be prepared.

Read Proverbs 6 and talk openly with your spouse about safeguarding your relationship together.

SEIZE THE ADVENTURE – Commit with Passion

"The God of all comfort, who comforts us in all our affliction, so that we may be able to comfort those who are in any affliction, with the comfort with which we ourselves are comforted by God."
2 Corinthians 1:3-4 (ESV)

TROUBLE IN THE CANYON – PART 2

After the second snake incident, we dusty hikers continued plodding down the canyon trail. With the heat rising and the sun now directly overhead, it was time to find some water. The team leader radioed to the rear guard and informed them he was getting off of the main trail to take a dip in the nearby creek. Unknown to all, large gaps had now separated each of the teams into three groups: the lead pack, the middle group and those in the back, who were marching at a slower pace.

When the final hikers arrived at the turn-off point to cool down in the refreshing stream and stock up on water for the last grueling portion of the hike the group was presented with a startling revelation. The middle team had not been informed of the change in plans. They'd, missed the turn-off and continued hiking and moving at a fast clip in hopes of catching the lead pack.

One of the men at the creek, Justin, a former Army Ranger, sprang into action. He took a radio, some water and after leaving his pack behind took off running, toward the separated hikers. The rest of the men took advantage of the time by playing in the creek. Thirty minutes later, a crackle came across the radio. "I've got good news and bad news." Justin had reached all three of the men in the middle group and was able to turn them around, but in the process he had twisted his ankle and broke his foot.

The team rallied around Justin, carrying his pack, offering trekking poles to aid in his painful walk to Phantom Ranch and the Ranger station. A female Ranger took a look at his ankle and foot, bandaged it and gave him ice to keep the swelling down. She laid out our options and we settled in for the night tending to Justin's needs as best we could. Because of his sacrificial act, he was now in pain and now dependent on God to get him out of this mess and to rely on the comfort and aid of his hiking group.

"We do not choose suffering simply because we are told to, but because the One who tells us to describes it as the path to everlasting joy." – John Piper

Tribulation and pain are normal occurrences in life and a person rarely escapes without enduring each a few times. As we go through these trials and suffering, God is there for us. Many times he will bring people into our lives who have suffered in a similar way, who can relate and bring comfort to us from their perspective. Some people turn their grief and heart-ache into ministry opportunities.

Is there someone you know that needs comfort?

Read 2 Corinthians 1, asking God for spiritual healing and list out people who need your help or comfort.

> "Count it all joy, my brothers, when you meet trials of various kinds, for you know that the testing of your faith produces steadfastness."
> James 1:2-3 (ESV)

TROUBLE IN THE CANYON – PART 3

Oh, how circumstances can change from good to bad in a hurry. In the morning we had enjoyed a beautiful descent into one of the greatest natural wonders of the world and now, in the evening, we found ourselves stuck at the bottom of the Grand Canyon. Our friend had a severely swollen ankle and a broken foot. There were three viable options. First, we could wait a couple of days for a helicopter to arrive, or second, take an uncomfortable mule ride to the top of the rim. The final option was to let him hike out on the broken foot.

To make matters worse, we had to sleep in an overflow area next to a cave filled with scorpions and a paddock of mules. The night was hot and smelly and the excitement from the day's events had made it difficult to sleep. I'm sure I could think of few better places to rest for the night, especially considering the circumstances.

The next morning we shook out our boots, ensuring that there were no scorpions hiding in them, and began the extremely slow an arduous hike up the South Rim. Justin had weighed his options and chose to hike out of the canyon, because it would take the helicopter two days to arrive and he figured the mule ride to the top would be just as excruciating as hiking out on his own. He was in a lot of pain, but he pressed on, taking it one step at a time. The team carried his back pack and worked together to get their wounded companion safely to the top.

"God never promises to remove us from our struggles. He does promise, however, to change the way we look at them." – Max Lucado

---

Justin missed out on the return trip back to the North Rim, but even though his trip had been cut short by his injury. He learned some valuable lessons. Justin learned what it is like to have God and others sustain him through a tough, physical and emotional trial. God is in control of all of our circumstances and He sustains. Whenever you find yourself facing a stretch of difficulty, lean on God, be open and honest with others and share your burdens, so they can come along side to help you through the pain.

When your faith is tested will you be ready and persevere?

Read James 1 and find a place of solitude. Pray and journal about how God has brought you through a tough time, or how you might respond when faced with an unwanted trial.

"Does he who supplies the Spirit to you and works miracles among you do so by the works of the law, or by hearing with faith – just as Abraham believed God, and it was counted to him as righteousness?"
Galatians 3:5-6 (ESV)

SUNKEN TREASURE

Diving into the dark and fast moving Au' Sable River allowed me to both be refreshed and also signal the beginning of our river tube float. When I pulled my head out of the water it hit me: I had just lost an expensive pair of sunglasses. They'd been sitting on top of my head but now most likely gone forever. Others joined me in searching for them, to no avail.

We enjoyed our two-hour float, and when it was over I returned to our starting point for one more attempt at finding my polarized sport glasses. The ladies in the group had been praying that I would find my sunken treasure, so I joined them in spirit and said a quick prayer before wading into the river and looked down. The sun appeared for a moment from behind a wall of clouds. Something on the river's bottom briefly reflected a ray of light and then disappeared. I dove in, expecting to pull out a piece of litter, but to my surprise I pulled out my lost sunglasses. God had answered our prayers.

"God's providence is not blind, but full of eyes." – John Greanleaf Whittier

The next day my truck broke down and I found myself stranded at a local gas station while the group I was leading was resting easy back at the cabins. God provided a man who towed the truck to his house, and another man who was able to get the parts to repair the truck from a shop over an hour away. In addition God touched the hearts of that same group of praying Christian ladies who, unsolicited, pitched in two hundred dollars to pay for the parts and labor. It was all done in perfect timing.

It was a weekend of small miracles that only God could have orchestrated. It is encouraging to be reminded that God cares about the day-to-day of life's troubles, no matter how small they seem or how big they become.

Do you pray to God even for the small things of life?

Begin to record your prayer requests and journal the details and events in life that you know only God could orchestrate. When you get discouraged, look back and see how God works.

> "What shall we say then? Are we to continue in sin that grace may abound? By no means! How can we who died to sin still live in it?"
> Romans 6:1-2 (ESV)

LOST IN THE MOUNTAINS – PART 1

It was difficult to sit back at camp while the rest of the hunting party dispersed into the mountains in search of elk. But the pain was excruciating and relentless, already having lasted two days. My body was dehydrated and worn out from the battle with a serious case of food poisoning and still suffered from its effects. Sometime around noon, I began to feel much better and decided I would head up a nearby trail into the mountains for a short and controlled hunt. This way, I could get back to camp quickly if necessary.

I left a note telling my father of my plans, grabbing my bow, a candy bar and a bottle of water on the way out. The trail was a moderate, but gradual climb to the top. It would take me a couple of hours to reach it, while stalking my prey. Upon arriving at the summit, I immediately consumed all of my water and the candy bar.

Searching for a place to recoup my energy, I ventured off of the trail. Fortunately, about a hundred yards down the side of the mountain; I found a muddy wallow in the dark timber. It was a perfect place to rest and wait for a visiting elk …

"The best way to fight against sin is to fight it on our knees." – Philip Henry

It seems that we entertain sin on a daily basis and then we are surprised when it hits us like a bad case of food poisoning. We flirt with temptation and then wonder why we are in a spiritual funk. Even though all things may be lawful, doesn't necessarily make them all profitable. Guard your heart, mind and body and protect your spiritual walk, by focusing on things in this world that encourage and uplift; not tear down and destroy. Don't let sin keep you from missing out on the great things God has planned for you.

Sins we give permission will eventually make us sick.

Read Romans 6, pray and confess your sins to God then make a plan to stop consuming things which make you sick.

> "Come to me, all who labor and are heavy laden, and I will give you rest. Take my yoke upon you, and learn from me, for I am gentle and lowly in heart, and you will find rest for your souls. For my yoke is easy, and my burden is light."
> Matthew 11:28-30 (ESV)

LOST IN THE MOUNTAINS – PART 2

Still suffering from the effects of food poisoning and a long hike, I sat perched on the side of a mountain behind some fallen logs; my temporary makeshift hunting blind was comfortable. It would provide the rest that I would need to finish out the day. The muddy wallow naturally created a circle shape opening in the forest, allowing for the afternoon sun to fill it with warmth. In between long and lazy blinks and the occasional head drop, I stared into the wallow and then into the surrounding woods. Searching and listening.

Finally a bull elk emerged from the dark timber, unannounced and cautious, as if looking for something, and then he stepped foot into the watery mud-hole. He was large and intimidating and seemed closer than he was. I slowly raised my bow and quickly fired a single arrow.

The arrow seemed to fly in slow motion, as it arced through the air towards the tan, majestic beast. As soon as the arrow struck him the elk took off running, fleeing in the same direction from which he had come. Excited, I set off in hot pursuit ...

> *"Christianity is a battle – not a dream." – Wendell Phillips*

There are times in life when you need to find rest. Living out the Christian life requires perseverance and endurance and there will be times when you just can't go on. That is ok, as long as we don't go backward in our walk. There are times we need to regroup, before pressing forward, and that should always be our primary goal. When we give ourselves rest even when we don't want to, God rewards us with the energy for what comes next. Often, rest goes against our nature but God knows all things and oversees our whole adventure. We only know what we can see in front of us.

In what or in whom will you find rest?

Read Matthew 11:25-30 and spend some time in solitude praying and seeking rest.

"For all have sinned and fall short of the glory of God." Romans 3:23 (ESV)

LOST IN THE MOUNTAINS – PART 3

The wounded elk was caught up in a pine tree. I silently moved in for a second shot in order to finish what I had started. The arrow flew straight. As I stood over the prize I came to the quick realization that the next step in the process was going to be too much for me to handle. I needed help.

Climbing to the top of the peak in search of the main trail, became somewhat of a challenge, since the elk lead me along a bowl shaped ridge through the dark timber and deposited me on a totally different mountain. The trail was nowhere to be found and for good reason.

There is a process people go through when they find themselves lost in the wilderness. I was just beginning Stage One. The first stage is denial. You deny the fact that you are lost …

"It is not sinning that ruins men, but sinning and not repenting, falling and not getting up again." – Matthew Henry

The Bible is very clear that there is no excuse or justifiable position for denying the existence of God. He has left his indelible mark on all of creation, including you and the intricate detail and care that he puts into helping you through life. Romans 1:20 says, "For his invisible attributes, namely, his eternal power and divine nature, have been clearly perceived, ever since the creation of the world, in the things that have been made. So they are without excuse." You're not lost, you're ignoring the Guide.

It is also very clear that we have all fallen short of God's holiness. No one is perfect, and everyone is lost without the saving power of Jesus Christ and having a personal relationship with Him. It is your right to deny this fact, but it doesn't change the reality of your situation. You are still lost.

Being lost is not adventure; it's just aimless wandering.

Read Romans 3:9-31. What does it say about us and where righteousness comes from?

"There is therefore now no condemnation for those who are in Christ Jesus for the law of the Spirit of life has set you free in Christ Jesus form the law of sin and death."
Romans 8:1-2 (ESV)

LOST IN THE MOUNTAINS – PART 4

Panic began to set in once I realized, I really was lost. This happens to be Stage Two of what people experience when they find themselves lost in the wilderness: panic, followed by a great sense of urgency to do something.

My emotions started whirling and a crazy thought raced through my mind: "Do I take off my underwear and cut it up into little strips to hang from tree branches, as a trail marker, so someone can find me?" Fortunately that thought quickly faded when I remembered my father telling me that if I ever found myself in an emergency situation that I should head southeast. He said I would be more likely to find a road in that direction. But, with panic setting in, I misunderstood his directions and went southwest, instead, deeper into the dark timber and mountainous wilderness of Colorado.

For many hours I hiked at a quick pace, having left the elk where it lay, descending into dark valleys and then ascending tall peaks. Darkness would soon approach. I was thirsty and tired from the previous battle with food poisoning, but with adrenaline coursing through me, there was no time or even reason to address that …

> *"It is vanity to mind only this present life, and not to make provision for those things which are to come."* – Thomas A. Kempis

Panic can affect you, whether you are spiritually lost, or just consumed with the burdens of life in general. It causes us to do things that we normally wouldn't do. Sometimes it is embarrassing and often times it is just the wrong thing to do. Instead of seeking advice from our heavenly Guide we look elsewhere. We seek out friends who give bad advice. We look to a messed up world hoping it has all of the answers.

Remember that panic is an emotional state, which indicates that you are starting to understand your predicament but that you just don't know what to do. Internal and external influences flood your system putting your mind and body into a whirlwind of confusion. God is peace. He is not confusion.

Who or what is at the foundation of your world view?

Are you tired of experimenting, hoping to fill the void?

Read Romans 8 and let God draw you to Him. Meditate on this chapter.

"Send out your light and your truth; let them lead me; let them bring me to your holy hill and to your dwelling!"
Psalm 43:3 (ESV)

LOST IN THE MOUNTAINS – PART 5

I was lost and still in Stage Two: Panic. It was early evening and darkness was setting in armed with only a very small flashlight, trekking through the dark timber and steep terrain would prove to be very difficult. Adrenaline kept me on the move for hours, but it wouldn't be long before I would eventually lose my light supply.

Hopeless and alone, in a deep valley, and facing a difficult climb with no light source remaining to guide my steps, I cried out, "Lord! I need your help." And then I prayed all of the way up a long and steep ascent. When I crested the top of a ridge; the moon illuminated a field of golden heather and a dusty two-track trail. The trail gave me a path to follow, but the moon was the lamp unto my feet.

"The voyage of discovery is not in seeking new landscapes, but in having new eyes." - Marcel Proust

Often, in life we find ourselves lost in a dark world, alone and without hope. Sometimes, it is the blackness of sin in our hearts and frequently, it is the darkness of the evil one that attempts to extinguish our light. Either way, we still find ourselves lost in the shadows of a world filled with evil, sin, and temptation. Repeatedly, we attempt to draw upon our own resources in hopes of meeting our misguided needs, but eventually find its illuminating power to be weak or that our own light source simply fades away.

Put your focus on the Light of this World, Jesus Christ and let his light and truth lead you to the top of the holy hill. Delve into the Scriptures and develop a consistent prayer life. Surround yourself with believers in Christ who can comfort, encourage and support you as you go back into the dark world to reach the lost.

Is Jesus Christ the lamp unto your feet?

Read John 8:12-30 and reflect on what Christ is saying about himself.

"I am the light of the world. Whoever follows me will not walk in darkness, but will have the light of life" – Jesus

> "Set your minds on things that are above, not on things that are on earth."
> Colossians 3:2 (ESV)

LOST IN THE MOUNTAINS – PART 6

The brilliance of the moon revealed a path that would lead me directly to Stage Three: It is here you formulate a new plan in hopes of correcting your out-of-control plight. My plan was to follow this path wherever it led, as long as it was downhill. I was tired, and I didn't want to climb any more mountains. Standing on the path, I chose to go the left. A few hundred yards away, I found myself standing at the bottom of one of the largest peaks in the area, Elkhorn Mountain. Remaining faithful to my new plan, I turned around and followed the easier path down the mountainside, and away from camp which was located on the same trail, just a few miles past this giant obstacle.

Sometime, long after midnight I collapsed on the trail. I could go no further. I had reached Stage Four: The physical and emotional breakdown when you realize that your new plan isn't working.

I built a fire in hopes of keeping warm on this cold mountain night. I tried to get some rest, but between keeping the fire fueled and fending off the local animal population, sleep would have to wait. The moon had settled in behind some clouds. It was pitch-black and I was alone.

> *"Spiritual darkness comes on horseback, and goes away on foot. It is upon us before we know that it is coming. It leaves us slowly, gradually, and not till after many days."* - J.C. Ryle

We often expend a lot of energy and emotion trying to formulate a new plan in order to solve our own spiritual condition. We spend a lot of time trying to do good works, seeking out other religions, or filling the void in our hearts with the pleasures of this world. But, the Bible is very clear that we are spiritually lost if we put our faith in these things. The more you try to fix your situation the more likely you are to remain lost. If you find yourself in stage three this is a good time to just rest and let God work in your life. Stop trying so hard to do it on your own.

What plan are you working under? Is your plan working?

Read Colossians 3, and find a place of solitude, meditate and rest.

"For God so loved the world, that he gave his only Son, that whoever believes in him should not perish but have eternal life." John 3:16 (ESV)

LOST IN THE MOUNTAINS – PART 7

A long, dark, and lonely night withdrew as the light of a new day shone brightly. It became abundantly clear, as the early morning light lit up the woods, that there was nothing I could do to be rescued. It was out of my control. I had entered Stage Five: Resignation to your plight and understanding that it will take someone else to save you. It is during this final stage that people choose to do whatever it takes to live or they do nothing and choose to remain lost, ultimately choosing death.

After a long morning hike, I finally reached the bottom of the mountain and stepped off of the trail and onto a dusty gravel road. I looked to my right and off in the distance, I could see a cloud of dust and a tiny car approaching. I flagged down the driver as he slowly approached and told him everything after he had stopped. I told him that I was sick, lost and that I didn't know my way back to camp. He said, "Son, I know where you are and I know how to get you home!"

Approaching camp we stopped my father, who was on his way to notify a search and rescue team of my situation. I could tell he was excited to see me, as he wrapped his arms around me in a powerful and loving embrace.

Now, would he believe I shot an elk?

"Eternal life is not a reward for effort; it is a gift to those who trust Christ."
- J. Vernon McGee

Later, it hit me that if I hadn't done something to flag him down I would still be lost. I had to step out into the middle of the road and wave my arms in a way that let him know that I was in trouble. He responded by safely escorting me back to the loving embrace of my father. Jesus Christ is waiting for you to resign yourself to the fact that there is nothing that you can do to save yourself, but that you too, just like me are in need of a heavenly Savior. No matter where you find yourself in your spiritual walk there are times when you need to flag down Christ and receive His help.

Salvation is God's gift and it is free, but in order to receive it you must first accept it.

Read John 3 and ask Jesus to be Lord and Savior of your life, if you haven't already done so.

"I am the Lord who heals you." Exodus 15:26 (ESV)

TANGLED BIRD

One night, I was called home early from leading an outdoor-ministry adventure. My mother was in the Intensive Care Unit fighting off a serious infection and had a dreadful day. I arrived home sometime after midnight, after a three hour drive. I spent the following morning in the hospital checking in on my mother and visiting with my father. It was an emotionally draining night and morning dealing with all of the emotion one experiences while watching a parent struggle with their health.

Later in the day, after the doctors upgraded her status to stable, I left the hospital to go home and mow the lawn. As my mower approached the badminton net, I noticed a bird twisted in the net. The bird was hanging upside down, tangled in a man-made net, struggling to get free.

I hoped off of the mower and grabbed a pair of gloves and a cutting tool. Gently clutching the bird's body and wings, I carefully began the process of untangling him. After freeing him, I delicately laid him on the ground and backed away. At that moment a song began to play and filled my ears with the most amazing message. The song was the *Healing Hand of God*, by Jeremy Camp. Like the bird, I, too, was tangled in a net, of emotion. Tears began to roll down my cheeks. It was the perfect song and great timing to be reminded of God's own infinite love and care.

"Where Love is, God is" – Henry Drummond

While, I was attempting to free the bird, he wasn't very cooperative and he kept trying to peck me with his beak. He resisted my help, even though I was being careful to keep him from harm. In the same way, God cares for us and loves us immensely. He is working to free us from the bondage of our sins and help us deal with the trials we face on a daily basis. He has a gentle, but firm grip on us, yet, many times we resist his help.

Relax and let the gentle hand of God, do His work.

Read Psalm 100 and know that His steadfast love endures forever.

> "Therefore, confess your sins to one another and pray for one another, that you may be healed. The prayer of a righteous person has great power as it is working."
> James 5:16 (ESV)

MOUNTAIN BIKE MUD BATH

It had been raining all week and the clouds showed no signs of leaving anytime soon. The mountain trails were filled with puddles and mud bogs. It was the perfect time to be mountain biking with a group of teens.

The young girls were a little nervous about riding in the mud, but after a few minutes their mud soaked bodies told them to just go for it and have some fun. They did and so did the rest of us. It turned out to be a great day and full of wet fun. We had memories to last a life time, but our clothes weren't as lucky.

Two of the senior boys in the group had taken the lead and disappeared out of sight. I was next in line and eventually caught up to them. Sitting on the side of the trail the two bikers looked concerned. I pulled up beside them to find out that one of the boy's bikes had a flat tire. This wasn't going to be an easy fix since none of us had ever changed out a flat tire on a mountain bike before. The other leaders took the rest of the teens to our final destination. The three of us stayed behind and worked on the bike together. It was difficult, but eventually we were able to get the bike back into action.

Taking the time to help them, though, meant that for some of us, the fun was over sooner than we'd hoped it would be.

"The greatest thing a man can do for his heavenly Father is to be kind to some of his other children." – Henry Drummond

---

Helping someone in need may be an inconvenience, but it's what our heavenly Father wants us to do. Ministry is about love, service and sacrifice. By our very nature we are designed for fellowship and community. We all want to be loved and to be able to show love. Real love is doing the things that you don't really want to do.

Seek out fellowship in a church and in a group of friends that you can share your troubles with and pray for each other. It's not necessarily about accountability; rather it is building strong family-like relationships to strengthen us in the body of Christ.

Are you willing to help someone out, even at a cost?

Read James 5:19-20 and then contact a friend who may have lost their way spiritually.

> "For no one can lay a foundation other than that which is laid, which is Jesus Christ."
> 1 Corinthians 3:11 (ESV)

WIDE OF THE MARK – PART 1

It was a cool, crisp and clear November afternoon. Conditions for bagging a monster whitetail were perfect. It was peak rut, virtually no breeze, and half a dozen doe were already spilling into the surrounding woods. A hunter couldn't ask for better circumstances.

All of the doe quickly snapped to attention and that is when I knew it was time. A giant eight-pointer sauntered into view; there was no need for an introduction. Everyone knew he was the "king of the woods". Focused and obsessed with his trophy rack, my thoughts drifted to an earlier conversation with my wife about where I would hang the prize in the house. I was hesitantly confident - my wife would agree that this might look best over our bed. I was wrong.

The buck jumped when the arrow pierced the ground just in front of him. Still unaware of where the sudden thud came from, the eight-pointer intent on finding an estrous doe pressed on. Armed with only two arrows, my next shot had to be on target.

"Unless we rely on God's power within us, we will yield to the pressures around us." – Anonymous

Sometimes we are distracted from the mark. Our focus no longer remains on what we are called to do; rather we get caught up in the flashy things life has to offer. We become more concerned with getting the trophy car, the trophy job or the trophy wife than earning these things and remaining humble. Our perspective becomes focused on the world, rather than developing an eternal perspective that guides our lives in a way that brings glory and honor to God, our Father in heaven.

Have you ever pursued trophies that caused you to be wide of the mark?

Read 1 Corinthians 3. Meditate on these verses and participate in a 24 hour fast (Liquids only). Every time you get hunger pains grab your Bible and read Scripture or take a few minutes and pray.

"I do not occupy myself with things too great and too marvelous for me. But I have calmed and quieted my soul."
Psalm 131:1-2 (ESV)

WIDE OF THE MARK – PART 2

The last arrow in the quiver took flight and sailed over the back of that four and a half year old eight-point buck. In an almost a mocking gesture, the mighty buck raised his shoulders and lifted his head high as he casually worked his way toward a nearby grazing doe. No longer armed, I sat helpless, and slowly watched him saunter to the other side of the woods and eventually out of sight.

I was so focused on his mighty rack that I was just about willing to do anything for a third chance. I climbed down from my tree-stand and with the stealth of a rhino I was able to reach my first arrow, presently stuck in the mud. Sitting on both knees, I yanked it out and was able to clean the broad head as I saw that familiar flash of white coming back in my direction. There was still hope.

A thirty-yard broad-side shot presented itself in just a matter of seconds. The arrow, back in flight again, raced towards the unsuspecting buck. The impact of the arrow ripped through the flesh of a little sapling tree before it came to a screeching halt. To my dismay I sat, lowly in the mud, watching the deer of my dreams literally and gracefully walk off into the sunset.

"Believe that you are defeated, believe it long enough, and it is likely to become a fact." – Norman Vincent Peale

It is a natural reaction to grasp at everything within our reach or letting loose with everything in our arsenal in hopes of hitting something when we try to do it all on our own. This becomes our strategy for overcoming the messes we make in our lives. We thrash, flash and clash in hopes of overcoming our mistakes, doing it all on our own power and with our own resources. Don't make a situation worse by continuing down the same path. Take a breath, relax, and be still.

Are you letting everything fly hoping something might stick?

Read Psalm 131 and take a day off from the hassles of life. Go and find a quiet place of solitude. Then relax, read, pray and meditate on God.

"Trust in the Lord with all of your heart, and do not lean on your own understanding. In all your ways acknowledge him, and he will make straight your paths." Proverbs 3:5-6 (ESV)

WIDE OF THE MARK – PART 3

It was a dark and gloomy day with forty to fifty mile an hour winds howling through the woods. Gun season was drawing near and the cold air was piercing. Immediately upon reaching my tree-stand, I caught a glimpse of a whitetail flag off in the distance. Did I scare off a new deer? No, it was the same Pope and Young eight-point buck dogging after a doe.

In our earlier encounter this whitetail trophy came out victorious, but this day would be different. My heart had changed. I knew what needed to be done. Years of training and experience quickly came flooding back. My focus no longer rested on boasting, or on the distraction of his mighty rack; instead my target became a matter of enjoying the hunt.

This time the mighty buck took my abilities for granted, taunting me by coming closer. I'm sure he thought he was safe since I had missed him three times earlier in the week. The impact of the arrow sent a shock wave through his body as the shaft of my arrow penetrated his heart. The "king of the woods" had now lost to a man who had learned to reset his priorities, resulting in a day of victory and redemption.

> "God never built a Christian strong enough to carry today's duties and tomorrow's anxieties piled on the top of them." — Theodore L. Cuyler

During perfect conditions I had easily missed the mark because my priorities were mixed up, but when I refocused and worried about what was important is when I had success, even during difficult conditions. I had lost sight and ignored years of training and practice, but when I changed my heart and my attitude I became victorious. God is not only a giver of second chances but unlimited chances. Reset the way you do things and let Christ be the focus of your life.

Where do the desires of your heart lie?

Read Proverbs 3:1-12 and break down these verses. Journal what this passage says to you?

"For as the lightning comes from the east and shines as far as the west, so will be the coming of the Son of Man." Matthew 24:27 (ESV)

MONSTER MISS

A loud bugle thundered through the tall aspens, bringing us to our knees. After looking at each other with big grins, the hunters quickly dispersed, and found cover. A twenty minute hike and our two week elk hunting trip would come to a close. The four of us were packed tightly together along the trail, as we casually walked and reminisced about our hunting adventures. It came when we were least expecting it and it came in the blink of an eye.

Drama was about to unfold. A regal, mature 6x6 bull elk, only one hundred yards away, charged towards our positions. The drop tines were something to behold, as well as the dark nature of the antlers, and the huge body of this sure to be record elk. It was the rut and this bull elk was spitting mad and ready for a fight with our skilled bugler. Rushing towards us at a quick pace the bull presented the first two hunters an opportunity, but each hunter passed as the monster of the woods headed right for the final shooter. Unprepared by the suddenness of the charging elk, his aim was off target and the opportunity of a lifetime was missed.

"Precisely because we cannot predict the moment, we must be ready at all moments." - C.S. Lewis

Scripture points to the rapture and the second coming of Christ and it all happens in the blink of an eye. It happens when we least expect it. The Bible says that no man knows the date or the time when it will happen, but that it will happen soon.

Life is busy, and it is filled with momentary pleasure. There is enough in this world to keep us preoccupied, but God wants us to be ready and to look forward to that special day, whenever it may be. It could be today, or maybe tomorrow.

Will you be ready and looking for the coming of Jesus Christ so you are not caught unprepared?

Read Matthew 24 and re-position your life to be ready for when He comes. While you're waiting fulfill the great commission and help those in need.

"For it is God who works in you, both to will and to work for His good pleasure."
Philippians 2:13 (ESV)

A NIGHT HIKE

The darkness disappeared as each man turned on his headlamp, illuminating the trail above. Like a military march of Cyclops, the hikers made their way through the wooded trail leading up to the highest point in the area, the Pinnacle, an old fire lookout tower. The Pinnacle has been known to be the host of many teenage parties over the years, but on this particular midnight clear there would be no rowdy drinking binges at the aged, dilapidated structure.

The breeze was refreshingly cool and the nighttime acoustics were perfect. After wiping the sweat from our brows, catching our breath, and downing a few liters of water, we began. The light of the full moon embraced the men as the opening prayer echoed in the darkness. I knew that this night would be no ordinary night; little did I realize how it would impact the rest of my life.

"This is the intersection we must cross: God begins with go, and we often begin with wait." – Erwin Raphael McManus

That night God gave to me the overwhelming desire to use his creation to connect men with one another, and draw people closer to

Christ. Shortly after this event I put myself in position to leave a corporate career and begin a new life of full-time ministry.

Being surrounded by God's embrace is a safe environment, but demands obedience and risk-taking. When we want to join God's amazing work we have no choice but to step out in faith and do the unimaginable. Don't stand in the way of God working through you. Relax, and let Him show you the way.

Are you waiting on God, or is He waiting on you?

Read Philippians 2 and brainstorm some possible ideas about how God could use you.

> "The wicked flee when no one pursues, but the righteous are bold as a lion."
> Proverbs 28:1 (ESV)

AFRAID OF GETTING HIT

Excitement was in the air. Everyone was ready for the season to begin. The football players dreamt of scoring a touchdown and winning their first game. But all of that would have to wait; the team still had a month of difficult and disciplined practice ahead of them. It would not damper their spirits, though. These youth were ready.

In the beginning of the practice season, players constantly asked to play running back or quarterback. They viewed these roles as high-profile glamour positions. The first two practices were without pads and everyone was having a great time running the ball and passing the ball. It looked like it was going to be a great season.

Then it came time to practice with full gear and pads. The players were ready to hit and tackle. The impact of the violent collisions could be heard and felt half-way across the field. Everyone was given the chance to run, and pass and face the dreaded defense. Slowly, one-by-one, players who had wanted to be in the game and who wanted to get the ball, said they no longer wanted to play the position anymore after getting hit. However, there were a couple of boys who couldn't get enough.

"Winners never quit and quitters never win." – Vince Lombardi

The Christian community is much like this football team. The church is excited to do God's work and to be called to do ministry. They like the idea of evangelizing the lost, supporting missionaries, and growing God's kingdom in various ways.

But sometimes, once the action begins, we find that the idea of doing ministry is much better than the reality of doing ministry. And when it actually comes down to getting dirty and committing to a life of love, service, and sacrifice many Christians ask to ride the bench. There are some who never want in the game, and some who quit after taking their first big hit. Others make it farther and then there are those who cannot get enough of serving God, doing whatever it takes.

Are you willing to take a hit for Christ?

Go to the back of the book and participate in the Faith Challenge Adventure, pray and ask God to reveal to you if you are for Him or just standing in the way.

SEIZE THE ADVENTURE – Commit with Passion

"I press on toward the goal for the prize of the upward call of God in Christ Jesus."
Philippians 3:14 (ESV)

A LEAP OF FAITH

After working my way to the edge of the giant boulder, I leapt off into the cool, dark water below. My two oldest children quickly followed, as soon as I gave them the thumbs up signal appeared indicating all was clear. However, my five year old son, Seth, was sitting with his mother begging and pleading with her to let him jump. She gently reminded him that he was too young and that it wasn't safe for him to try. After all, other kids twice his age were chickening out, one by one, in front of him. Seth persisted and we insisted. I reinforced his mother's decision; I, too, was leery about his ability to jump.

The crowd gathered this hot summer day watched the situation with interest. Seth continued and finally wore us down. I held his hand and lead him to the edge of the giant boulder positioned over the lake, which was a perfect natural diving platform. I jumped in and then tread water ten feet below my son. I could see the resolute face of a champion who then jumped to thunderous applause. The awestruck gallery of previously failed participants was clearly impressed by the actions of this one small jumper.

"All God's giants have been weak men who did great things for God because they reckoned on His being with them." – James Hudson Taylor

If you want to "Seize the Adventure" that God has for your life you must first put aside the negative feedback of those who say that it cannot be done. Next, you must press forward and climb over the obstacles that life puts in your way and then take a leap of faith, emerging victorious. Not only did a small boy accomplish something great for himself, but because of his efforts, he inspired others to step out and take a risk. A five year old child became a leader on this day, and led others to experience a life of excitement and reward.

Does your faith-walk inspire others?

Read Philippians 3 and take a few minutes to pray, asking God to show you how your life could inspire others to follow Him.

> "Lead me in your truth and teach me, for you are the God of my salvation; for you I wait all the day long."
> Psalm 25:5 (ESV)

LURE PIERCING

Conditions were perfect for fishing. The weather cooperated and the small lake teemed with fish. On a previous trip to this same lake, my father had caught a giant Tiger-Muskie, so expectations were high. Everything was set for spending a great evening fishing with my father, hopefully living out memories that would last a life time.

Using the oars that came with the boat, my father paddled us into position near the small dam. We opened up our tackle boxes, put on our best lures, and after spraying for mosquitoes, we were set. Nothing left to do, except fish.

I opened up the bale and reached the pole back as far as I could. I looked to cast the lure as far as possible. Focusing straight ahead and looking at the optimal fishing spot, I thrust my pole forward as fast and as hard as a young child could muster. My pole snapped back. It would not move forward. I was snagged on something, determined to free it, I kept yanking it, hoping it would somehow free itself. It wasn't until my father finally was able to let out a scream and crash across the boat that I realized I had hooked him in the ear, piercing him with my three-pronged lure!

"Pride is at the bottom of all great mistakes." – John Ruskin

We boated back to town where the doctor was able to remove the hook from his pierced ear with a pair of pliers. I felt terrible, but my father was gracious through the whole ordeal. Had he thrown me overboard, he would have been justified.

Have you ever tried to force something to happen? Often we try to force God's hand in a particular situation, hoping to get our desired results. Everything is situated just right. Everything is perfect, but something seems to be holding us back, yet we go to great lengths to try and free it on our own without first figuring out what the problem is.

When God snags are you still fighting?

Read Psalm 25 and reflect on how God used a snag in your life for good.

"For God is not a God of confusion but of peace."
1 Corinthians 14:33 (ESV)

SHOOTING FRENZY

My father and I were out hunting mule deer in the rolling hills of Wyoming. As we came up a draw three bucks and some doe ran down a rise in front of us. Picking out our trophies, we began to shoot. This sent the deer into a state of pandemonium. Deer were running every which way and both my dad and I became confused as to which deer we had shot at. One of the bucks lay dead at the bottom of the ravine, and another one ran up the other side of the hill. I shot, hitting the deer a couple of times, but it wouldn't be stopped. My gun jammed, so my father sat down and steadied his gun on his knee, dropping the mule deer with the precision of a military sniper.

> *"We live in a troubled age. For every problem that has a solution, there is a solution that brings another problem. Few know where we are headed, but universally acknowledge that we are careening along at break neck speed."*
> – Richard A. Swenson, M.D.

So who shot which buck? Who really knows for sure? After some discussion and rational guesses, we tagged our deer but neither of us really knew what had just gone on. Graciously, my father let me have the biggest rack.

Like the deer outside influences and people create confusion in our lives. What can we do about it? What should we do about it? Sometimes the disorder in life is brought about because of our bad choices and other times it comes without any purpose or even warning. Be encouraged we have a God who is an expert at sorting out the turmoil we create.

Is your life filled with confusion and pandemonium?

Find a quiet getaway and pray and meditate on what really is important in your life. Ask God to show you what you can cut out of your hectic schedule.

"By this we know love that he laid down his life for us, and we ought to lay down our lives for our brothers."
I John 3:16 (ESV)

STUCK UNDERWATER – PART 1

Our whitewater rafting trip was nearing its end. The final rapid was all that stood in the way of a successful run down the raging river. This particular rapid presented us with two options for possible escape. The way right looked fun, but not all that challenging. The way left more difficult, but would provide the people in our raft a series of waves that would certainly guarantee a great finish. But choosing this second option would require us to navigate between two giant boulders acting as the river's gatekeepers.

Our straight-line approach was perfect until an unseen boulder turned our raft and sent us slamming into the two unmovable objects, sideways. My future wife was ejected from the raft and into the icy-cold water and quickly slid underneath. The raft pressed against the rocks by the force of the water and blocked the passageway. My instincts took over; realizing she was pinned underwater I jumped in to save her. I'd attempted a daring rescue but soon found out that I, too, was a victim. I crashed into her. She felt cold and limp. I wrapped my arms and legs around her, struggling to pull us free from the overwhelming power and force of the mighty water slamming into us from behind. I knew that my life might be forfeit now, too.

"The man without a purpose is like a ship without a rudder – a waif, a nothing, a no man." – Thomas Carlyle

---

God wants us to love Him and to love others and if we keep His commandments He abides in us. He wants us to love the unlovable, serve people in need, and sacrifice parts of our life in order to serve Him. After all, God made the greatest sacrifice of all, by giving up His Son to satisfy God's wrath and pay the price for our sins.

Are you willing to let go of a lucrative career to step into a ministry position? Would you move to another state or country to answer His call? What would you be willing to sacrifice for the sake of God's calling on your life?

How does a life of love, service and sacrifice look for you?

Read 1 John 3 and reflect on how many times the word love is used in this chapter.

"Save me, O God! For the waters have come up to my neck. I sink in deep mire, where there is no foothold; I have come into deep waters, and the flood sweeps over me." Psalm 69:1-2 (ESV)

STUCK UNDERWATER – PART 2

While my fiancée and I were stuck in the river the two men still remaining in the troubled raft began to panic. What could they do to save their two friends stuck below in the frigid river? Two cold and wet bodies pressed up against the bottom of the raft, pinned by the force of the raging whitewater. There was no escape, stuck literally between a rock and a hard place. Hope began to fade.

Then in an instant our troubles disappeared. A rush of water swept over us, pushed us through the boulders, and into a series of punishing waves and rapids. It took one of the men to finally realize that his own body weight was keeping the boat lodged in place. Tackling the other man shifted the weight enough to cause the raft to heave, removing the obstacle in our path. In that instant we were swept away by an act of grace.

"He giveth more grace when the burdens grow greater, He sendeth more strength when the labors increase; to added affliction He addeth His mercy, to multiplied trials, His multiplied peace." - Annie Johnson Flint

The demands of work, financial stress, pressures of marriage and children, and the responsibilities of serving in church can sometimes lead to moments of feeling overwhelmed – pinned between a rock and a hard place with no escape. Keeping up with a fast-paced life is difficult and not healthy for your family and spiritual life. Like the man in the raft we need to shift our weight and re-evaluate our position in life and reduce the craziness in our schedules.

Say No! What can you eliminate from your busy schedule?

Read Psalm 69 and pray that God's grace would be enough for you today. Take some time and journal. List out all of your tasks and then prioritize them. Then eliminate what is not important.

SEIZE THE ADVENTURE – Commit with Passion

"Now Jesus loved Martha and her sister, and Lazarus. So, when he heard that Lazarus was ill, he stayed two days longer in the place where he was." John 11:5-6 (ESV)

SITTING THE BENCH

I grew up in a family of outdoor enthusiasts. Adventure was always on the horizon for our family. Camping, fishing, and hunting were many of our favorites, but my special love was always baseball.

My baseball skills were legendary, in my own mind at least, but allowed me many years on the field of play. It was fun and exciting. In other sports I learned how to sit the bench, but in baseball I was always able to avoid that disappointment. Baseball was my passion and my future. However, youthful dreams eventually give way to bigger ambitions, in my case, a life of ministry.

Like in baseball, my ministry experiences have been similar in that I have always been fortunate to be actively in play. God has sought to use me in various positions over time. But recently I have become familiar with sitting on the ministry bench as I've waited for God to move me into my next phase of ministry. Honestly, it has been difficult at times. I want to get back in the game, but for some reason the Coach has determined it is better for me to ride the pine.

"Faith sees the invisible, believes the unbelievable, and receives the impossible."
— Corrie Ten Boom

Should we question the Coach? No. He knows the plan he has for us and we have to trust Him. His timing is always perfect. When a coach puts a player on the bench it is often to teach them something about what they've been doing or about something that will help them be better. It is also a technique used to get a player refreshed and recharged, so they can be effective when going back into the game.

Waiting patiently on God is hard but essential to a enjoying a peaceful and joyful life. Let Him prepare the way. He may be giving you this unique opportunity to enjoy your family, before the rush of life consumes again. Praise the Lord for the example he set when He created the world and rested on the seventh day.

Do you think there are reasons why God is delaying?

Read John 11 and see if you can pick out the reasons why Jesus delayed during this time of need in Lazarus' life. What did the Disciples learn? How about Mary? And what did Martha discover?

SEIZE THE ADVENTURE – Commit with Passion

"Now there are varieties of gifts, but the same Spirit; and there are varieties of service, but the same Lord; and there are varieties of activities, but it is the same God who empowers them all in everyone."
1 Corinthians 12:4-6 (ESV)

SUPERNATURAL DESIGNER

On a recent family vacation to Washington D.C., I was amazed at the creativity of man, but overwhelmed by our Creator. On the second day of our trip, we visited the White House and went to the top of the Washington Monument, both worthy examples of man's creative genius. However, they were not without visible flaws and needed repairs.

Later that day we were able to hear an expert at the National Zoo share the amazing and flawless design of a cheetah, God's creative genius. He explained the features which allow it to be a great hunter and the fastest animal on the planet. God gave Cheetah's special claws for running, but not climbing, a sleeker skull with a smaller mouth and a larger nostril cavity to pull in more oxygen for running purposes, as well as the right kind of limbs, spine, and muscles needed to hunt its prey at high speeds. Later we listened to another individual share with us the purpose and design of feathers for great birds of flight. After a lengthy explanation, I was slightly amused when he told my children that man really didn't know why or how the feathers were designed in this special way.

"A man can no more diminish God's glory by refusing to worship Him than a lunatic can put out the sun by scribbling the word, 'darkness' on the walls of his cell." – C.S. Lewis

The imagination of man is filled with a conundrum of thoughts, a plethora of visions and contradicting plans to do both good and evil. The mind of man is restless, but pure in his own mind. It is bold, proud, arrogant and boastful, yet a vast sea of doubt, insecurity and fear. The mind is a mystery to its owner, but not to its incredible designer.

Man doesn't have all of the answers, but God, our loving creator does. He has a purpose and a design for everything He makes, including you, and the plans He has for your life. Are you willing to surrender your life to Him and trust Him with the plan He has for your life?

How has God wired you? What are your gifts?

Journal and make a list of the spiritual gifts that you believe God has given you. Next, go and ask three people who know you really well, spiritually, to list your gifts and strengths. Then compare.

"Now Faith is the assurance of things hoped for, the conviction of things not seen. For by it the people of old received their commendation." Hebrews 11:1-2 (ESV)

A MAN OF FAITH

With a harness securely wrapped around me there shouldn't have been any cause for concern. The rope was thick enough. The buckles were secure and snugged tightly. My helmet was fastened on my skull and the body was willing, but my mind was lagging a bit behind. Could I just step off the edge of a cliff?

"Just lean out and step off!" The rock-climbing guide instructed.

Yea Right! But in order to seize a life of adventure a person must be willing to let go of what his mind is telling him, trust in his gear, his guide and enjoy the experience of doing something that makes absolutely no sense, like repelling off a steep cliff.

"The reward of being faithful over a few things is just the same as being faithful over many things; for the emphasis falls upon the same word; it is the faithful who will enter into the joy of their Lord." – Charles S. Robinson

A weak man of faith walks by himself, but a strong man of faith walks securely with God. A solid man of faith may not totally understand the path that God lays out before him, but he is still up for the challenge. A soft man of faith robs himself of adventure and blessing by avoiding the pain and the struggle inherent in the journey. A man unyielding in his faith understands his own thoughts are rather shallow, but that God's thoughts are never ending in depth. An acquiescent man of faith is a slave to his fear and doubts.

Men of faith do not worry about qualifications, but faithless men are consumed with their resumes. When it comes to making a difference in this world for God, men of faith see a God of limitless power and faithless men see only the limitations within themselves. When men fully grasp that they are nothing and God is everything is the moment when one's faith begins to head in a new direction.

Man without a strong faith settles for a mediocre life, but a man with great faith is built for adventure.

What kind of faith do you desire? Is your faith weak or strong?

Build your faith in prayer and by reading about the men and women of faith in Hebrews 11.

"In you, O Lord, do I take refuge; let me never be put to shame! In your righteousness deliver me and rescue me; incline your ear to me, and save me!" Psalm 71:1-2 (ESV)

A DIVINE SOTER

My wife and I were walking hand in hand, romantically strolling down a sidewalk, and enjoying the final moments of our anniversary getaway. We casually approached a pet store and a sign caught our attention, which stated, "Rescue pet adoptions inside." The first words out of my wife's mouth were, "We are not getting a dog!"

"A hmm."

As our wonderful weekend came to an end we were both grateful for the time spent alone and away from our five children, but we were also excited to see them again. And to show them our brand new puppy! Over the course of a few hours both parents and children set out to discover the perfect name for our new full-breed mutt. My wife came up with the idea to give him a name that represented salvation, since we had rescued him. Our first name, Salvo (An Italian word for saved) sounded cool, but many of the younger children had trouble pronouncing it clearly, so we continued our name quest.

"Since every aspect of salvation is solely the work of God, it cannot possibly be lost." – John MacArthur, Jr.

Finally, the name Soter was chosen which in the Greek language means savior, deliverer, or preserver. Life is short and the only thing certain in it, besides taxes is that we are all appointed to die. This puppy had an appointment with death, but was rescued. His name is the perfect reminder of our own mortality and our need of spiritual rescue from a Divine Soter. His name is Jesus Christ.

Have you ever rescued anything or been rescued?

How did you feel about it?

Read Psalms 71 and 72 and find a place of solitude to praise your Creator.

"And he awoke and rebuked the wind and said to the sea, 'Peace! Be still!' And the wind ceased, and there was a great calm. He said to them, 'Why are you so afraid? Have you still no faith?'" Mark 4:39-40 (ESV)

FLASH FLOOD

Everyone was tired from a week of mountain biking, whitewater rafting, rock climbing, and rappelling. All of the teens were tucked away in their tents for the night and it was remarkably quiet. The trip had been challenging both physically and spiritually, but the fun wasn't over yet.

The first incident came just before midnight when a tent filled with boys and snacks attracted the attention of a couple of curious skunks. I was awakened to shouts of false bravado as they attempted to scare off the hungry critters, to no avail. After saving the boys from their fearless attackers, I nestled back into my sleeping bag and fell asleep to the sound of a light rain.

A few hours later, I was startled by the shouts of more youth yelling, waking everyone in our group. I went outside in the pouring rain and brought some calm to the frantic and soaked youth. I quickly realized that all of their tents had been flooded. The rain intensified even more and after a week of rain, conditions were perfect for flash flooding, forcing all of us to head to the nearest hotel for the night. Flooding in the area was widespread and a few deaths had resulted from the deluge but not in our group.

"Before me, even as behind, God is, and all is well." – John Whittier

Leaders in ministry are susceptible to getting washed out. The demands and pressures of ministry are more than most lay people even know. Spiritual leaders are given authority to lead and shepherd the church, but are also held more spiritually accountable. The evil one is looking to make the life of Christian leader difficult and making sure his life is full of temptation, hoping he fails.

Pray for your leaders and encourage them to take some rest once in a while. Come along side of them and love them. They are people too and they may need some affirmation, or extra encouragement. Do something special for them. If you are in leadership talk to other staff or your elders and discuss setting up ways to prevent wash out.

How can you keep your faith from getting washed out?

Read Mark 4:35-41 and take a few minutes thank Christ for having the power over all things and that he protects, sustains and keeps us from washing out.

SEIZE THE ADVENTURE – Commit with Passion

"But, as it is written, what no eye has seen, nor ear heard, nor the heart of man imagined, what God has prepared for those who love him."
1 Corinthians 2:9 (ESV)

LUCKY SHOT

The morning hunt produced very little. It was a cold, brisk mid-November afternoon. Fortunately, we were not still hunting in a frigid tree-stand, but actively pursuing our quarry with a method known as driving deer or pushing deer.

Three quarters of the way through our final wood-lot a buck appeared on my side of the woods, about seventy five yards ahead of me. He ran to the end of the trees and into an open field. I pressed after him, running with my partner right behind me. We approached the open field, but the deer was now nowhere to be seen. Continuing forward, we slowly walked through the field, knowing that he had to have lain down somewhere. Slowly progressing through the weeds, we could now see a small ditch about a hundred yards ahead.

Suddenly the deer shot up and out of the ditch, running parallel to me and my hunting partner. We both opened fire on the fleeing buck. Alternating shots could be seen hitting the snow on the ground all around the deer as the deer continued to run. Down to my final shot, I dropped to one knee and readjusted. The deer turned directly away from me as I squeezed the trigger. The final roar from the shotgun brought disbelief from the other hunters looking on from a nearby hill. The deer had dropped immediately. Shocked, we paced off the distance and it came to be a one hundred and eighty-five yard shot.

"For the Christian, there are, strictly speaking, no chances. A secret Master of the Ceremonies has been at work." - C.S. Lewis

Some say it was a lucky shot. I prefer to say that it was a skill shot. The kind of shot that is only taken by trained snipers, but for some reason my friends laugh at that comment and I grin along with them. Lucky or not it was still a memorable hunt.

With God behind you, your life is not a coincidence.

Read 1 Corinthians 2 and begin to journal your prayer requests and the ways God is working in your life. Looking back, you will easily see that it is not coincidence.

"You shall not take the name of the Lord your God in vain, for the Lord will not hold him guiltless who takes his name in vain." Exodus 20:7 (ESV)

LUNCH TIME STALK

Even when I'm inside my house, I am always hunting for whitetail deer. My favorite hunting blind, besides my tree-stand, is our family's breakfast nook. With six windows and plenty of heat, it is the perfect place to view deer on our property.

One afternoon I'd just sat down to lunch when I looked out the window and noticed some white branches in the woods that looked oddly out of place. I grabbed my binoculars and noticed that it was not branches, but the giant eight-pointer I had been hunting all season! He was bedded down about seventy-five yards from the house. I handed the binoculars to the children and told them to keep watch. I threw on some boots, an orange vest, and grabbed the shotgun I've had since I was a teenager.

I bolted out the front door and moving to the backyard, I began to stalk the monster deer. As I made my way, I'd often glance back at the house where the kids would occasionally give me thumbs up indicating the buck was still there. Slipping down into the creek ditch, I climbed up the other side and positioned myself for a shot. I squeezed the trigger and the gun recoiled against my shoulder. The buck jumped and hopped over a fallen tree. I fired off another round, but no luck.

"We have a strange illusion that mere time cancels sin." – C.S. Lewis

---

I spent hours trying to force the result that I wanted, but to no avail. My gun is designed for shooting birds and it does not have a rifled barrel, therefore it shoots deer slugs high and to the left. Once I was in the heat of battle, I forgot to compensate for this problem when I put the bead on my intended target. That was the third big buck that I missed as a result of using that gun. Needless to say, I'm getting another gun.

Christians often find themselves committing the same mistakes over and over again. However, it's time to stop doing the things that we know are wrong and the things that have consequences and then expect God to fill our lives with blessing. Is it time for a new gun?

Are you doing things wrong, but still hoping for good results?

Read Exodus 20 and reflect on which of the Ten Commandments you continually break.

"My soul finds rest in God alone; my salvation comes from him. He alone is my rock and my salvation; he is my fortress, I will never be shaken."
Psalm 62:1-2 (NIV)

MONSOON SEASON

A compass. A map of the Grand Canyon. A pad of paper and a pencil lay. There was excitement in the room, as the couples poured over the details of the adventure and the path they were about to take. Every aspect of the adventure was carefully thought out and poured over with painstakingly detail.

This hiking trip was different; four couples instead of eight men embarked on their journey to the bottom of the Grand Canyon, enjoying every moment and taking in all of the sights and sounds. Everything was going as planned, with the exception of the heat. Hiking in July is already a challenging endeavor, but the severe and unexpected rise in temperatures only increased the level of difficulty. It would take all day to get to the bottom and set up camp. The heat had been miserable, but overall the experience in the canyon was breathtaking. Soaking in the cold river and hiking to Rainbow Falls were some of the highlights and helped make the heat-wave more tolerable. It was already going to be a memorable excursion, but they weren't prepared for what would happen next.

All that remained of their adventure was the challenging and final ascent out of the canyon. The team was a little more than half-way up the South Rim when a severe and unexpected thunderstorm rolled over the South Rim. Fortunately, the exhausted hikers had reached one of the few shelters along the Bright Angel trail and huddled together, fearing for their own safety as water poured down the sides of the canyon. Other hikers were caught out on the trail and left vulnerable to the ferocious weather. The roar of thunder was deafening and lightning was everywhere. To make matters worse, hail began to fall from the angry sky as rock and debris slid down the sides of the canyon, creating mudslides. The canyon was under attack and the scared hikers were helpless. They clung to each other as other hikers crammed into the shelter seeking relief from the storm. There was a real potential for death in the canyon that day, but all members of the hiking group rode out the storm and made it out alive.

"Suffering passes, but the fact of having suffered never leaves us." - Leon Bloy

Every now and then life forces us to hunker down. Rain is inevitable, but occasionally a monsoon hits, halting us in our tracks. It is in times like these when we need to seek shelter, regroup, lean on friends and family and draw strength from our faith in Christ.

**God is a refuge for us.
Trust in Him at all times.**

Read Psalm 62, pray for God's protection over your life and remember that no matter what comes your way, God is your rock and your fortress. Find shelter in Him.

Adventure Notes:

Prayer Journal: Yes No Grow

"Evil men do not understand justice, but those who seek the Lord understand it completely." Proverbs 28:5 (ESV)

NO RECORD

The master of ceremonies came to the podium to announce the final standings of the competition and whether or not any records were broken. When he announced that there was a new record in the agility race, I got my video camera ready. I knew that my son had clearly been the fastest runner on the course. I clicked the camera's start button in anticipation of filming this great moment in my young boy's life.

As the announcer called the name of another child my heart was broken. It was a travesty! An injustice as far as I was concerned, but my son handled it in a very mature manner. I was sure Zach had won because the year before he had come really close to breaking the record and he ran an even better race this time. His coach anticipating a record-breaking performance had even timed his race, giving us an all's good signal at the end of the race.

I, on the other hand, couldn't let it go, so I went home and reviewed the video, over and over, even breaking it down in slow motion. My investigation proved that my son had indeed set the agility record. The home video showed that the official time keeper was slow in his response when stopping the watch.

"All roads lead to the judgment seat of Christ." – Keith Green

Although my son wasn't recognized for breaking the record he can live with the fact that he ran a great race. Even though there was an injustice in the keeping of time, he still is a winner in his father's eyes. His feat is not diminished because he did not get the earthly glory that he deserved.

There are times in life when injustice prevails. When those who do wrong reap rewards or get the better positions. Sometimes evil triumphs over good and men with integrity are slandered by fools filled with sin. Don't lose heart; there is hope and there will be a time coming soon when injustice will finally be put to rest in God's perfect timing.

Are you willing to let go of your life's biggest injustice?

Read Psalm 106 and pray and wait on God and let Him right the injustices in your life.

> "Whoever trusts in his own mind is a fool, but he who walks in wisdom will be delivered." Proverbs 28:26 (ESV)

DOWNHILL CRASH

If you like drama and lots of action then go on a two-week family vacation. You won't be disappointed. Family outings are the perfect situations in which to build up unity, but also create some long and lasting memories. The experienced vacationer knows and understands this, and yet despite this knowledge goes back for more.

Travelling with a young child is a test of patience. Bring that total up to five and it becomes an extreme adventure. The first memorable moment on a recent trip came fifteen minutes in when a loud wail echoed throughout the mini-van. It was the cry of our one-year-old daughter. Her cry finally ended ten hours later upon arrival at our final destination – Wisconsin side of Lake Michigan.

Our camp site was nestled on a small hill in the woods along the edge of its sandy shoreline. It was the perfect day to swim and build sandcastles. My wife and I loaded up a push cart filled with beach essentials: towels, toys, chairs, games, lunch, and our one-and-two-year-old daughters.

As I pushed the cart downhill it began picking up speed and a playful instinct took over. I whooped with excitement and the girls began to laugh, as we descended down the hill. The laughing soon turned to horror as the wheels of the push cart collapsed and sent myself and both girls flying through the air. A moment of fun and careless thinking forced us to miss a full day at the beach and spend an afternoon visiting an emergency room for a tweaked ankle, seven stitches and general humiliation.

"Pride is at the bottom of a great many errors and corruptions, and even of many evil practices, which have a great show and appearance of humility."
– Matthew Henry

Often we live our lives for the moment and in doing so we open ourselves up for regrettable situations and in some cases, public humiliation. Think about the consequences of your actions next time you find yourself in a tempting situation! The effects of our sins don't just impact us but they often ripple outward hurting other people along its path of destruction.

Have the consequences of your sins affected others?

Read Proverbs 28 and meditate on your past sins. Have you confessed your sins to God? Have your sins hurt other people? Have you gone to them to make matters right and seek forgiveness?

"For my thoughts are not your thoughts, neither are your ways my ways, declares the Lord. For as the heavens are higher than the earth, so are my ways higher than your ways and my thoughts than your thoughts."
Isaiah 55:8-9 (ESV)

LEAVING THE TRAIL EARLY

The early signs of darkness began to creep into the woods, placing a hush over all that inhabited it. Being a stranger to this woodland community, I began to get a little nervous. The surroundings were unfamiliar and the silence was intimidating. I decided that I would be leaving early.

When I was twelve years old my father took me bow hunting and placed me in a temporary ground blind along a deer trail, deep in the woods. My father left me and went further into the forest. After a couple of hours with no sign of deer, and the daytime sky beginning to show signs that its time had come to an end, put fear and doubt into my heart. I left the strategic position of the deer blind and decided to sit fifty yards away on the main trail, feeling somewhat safer for having done this. Ten minutes later, looking back on my previous location, I soon realized my mistake when I witnessed three deer standing only fifteen feet from where I sat. I had blown it. I would not get an opportunity to shoot. All I could do was stand quietly and watch as the very thing I was pursuing was now out of reach.

"Failures are finger posts on the road to achievement." – C.S. Lewis

How many times do we find ourselves feeling uncomfortable in our current surroundings and decide to bail? How many times have we missed out on the blessings of what God has planned for us, because we get scared at the first sign of opposition?

We serve a remarkable God whose ways are much higher than ours. Don't let the people in your life or in your church limit God. Don't be afraid when God places you in unfamiliar surroundings. He has an intentional plan and He understands everything in it. His sovereignty over all things will make sure of that, so don't fret. Even when the darkness creeps in; God has you where he wants you. Let him be your light and your guide.

God's responsible for His plans.
Your role is obedience.

Read Isaiah 55 and that accomplishes his purposes. Take this time to journal your thoughts about where you think God is going to take you or how he could use you and list out your prayer requests.

"The heart of man plans his way, but the Lord establishes his steps." Proverbs 16:9 (ESV)

THE RECRUIT

In my first year as a varsity baseball coach I told the players that I would learn as much from them as they would learn from me. That statement would ring true by the end of the season. One of our players was being scouted by a Big Ten school and one of their scouts would be showing up to watch our star player, Tommy Jablonski. The pressure was on and it definitely showed. Our team was easily defeated in five quick innings, per the Michigan high school mercy rule. It took us longer to drive to the game than it did to actually play the game. Our team leader played well, but not up to the high standards of our Division 1 school scout.

Would it be the end of his baseball dream? No. Sure his disappointment could be felt by all of us, but God would use him to deliver a message that God is in control of our lives. Afterward, Tommy was able to speak to a large group at a local church about his baseball setback. He shared about letting go and trusting God to work out the details of his life.

"Without counsel plans fail, but with many advisers they succeed."
- Proverbs 15:22 ESV

Tommy would go on to be signed by another Division 1 school and would eventually work through injury to become a team leader in both his leadership off of the field and in his play on the field.

Are you willing to give control of your life over to God? Are you ok with God having sovereignty over your life? It may not always look the way we want it to, or turn out the way we hope, but if we let God have control over every aspect of our life, our earthly setbacks will ultimately have eternal results.

Let God use your setbacks for His glory and keep pressing on.

Find a place of solitude and meditate on God's Word. Give God permission to guide your steps in life. Read Proverbs 16.

"…More than that, we rejoice in our sufferings, knowing that suffering produces endurance, and endurance produces character, and character produces hope…"
Romans 5:3-4 (ESV)

THROUGH THE DARKNESS – PART 1

Unable to penetrate the thick blanket of fog and clouds, the sun remained hidden for the day. The weather wasn't the only challenge the men would face this day. There are some days that just start off wrong, but today, it was done by design.

Emerging from their frost covered tents, the men were tired and sore from whitewater rafting the day before, but still assembled for the morning hike. The men were given a granola bar for breakfast and one military M.R.E. meal which would be their only food source for the entire day. The men were not happy to say the least. The group was broken into evenly matched teams. Each squad would receive a handheld G.P.S. unit to assist them in finding four caches spread out around the mountains. Three out of the four caches held the same items, sauerkraut, sardines, and a couple of other uninteresting food items. The fourth cache would be found in a padlocked black container. The teams were to bring the locked container back to camp.

After a grueling hike and the challenge of finding the worthless caches the men grew even wearier and the grumbling flourished. The men were given a short break and some men ate their only meal and others chose to wait. The adventure closed with a cave excursion and cold swim exiting the cave.

Upon exiting the cave the men gathered around the campfire, heard a short devotional about the purpose of the day's events, and then were extremely excited when they opened up the padlocked containers and feasted on all of the goodies placed inside of them. What began as a dismal, painful and difficult day ended with a night full of praise and a cache full of great reward. Their mood had changed.

"Mystery is but another name for our ignorance; if we were omniscient, all would be perfectly plain." – Tryon Edwards

Sometimes we are faced with life-situations that we don't necessarily want to be a part of. It may be a physical challenge, or a spiritual test. We may have to carry the burden of confronting a friend who is caught up in sin, or try to evangelize with an atheist, who is a great debater. God uses difficult and trying situations to grow us and to teach us more about him. A life of perseverance and endurance will lead us to a life of eternal reward.

SEIZE THE ADVENTURE – Commit with Passion

Sometimes what God asks of us is not always glamorous?

Read Romans 5, and reflect on the peace we can have with God through our faith.

Adventure Notes:

Prayer Journal: <u>Yes</u> <u>No</u> <u>Grow</u>

_____
_____
_____
_____
_____
_____
_____
_____

SEIZE THE ADVENTURE – Commit with Passion

"I have fought the good fight, I have finished the race, I have kept the faith."
2 Timothy 4:7 (ESV)

THROUGH THE DARKNESS – PART 2

The men had finished the hiking portion of the day and now it was time for the cave exploration. A river rushed into the hole in the side of the mountain. The entrance to the cave was dim, but once the men were no more than fifty feet inside the earthen tunnel became pitch black. It was so dark inside that each man had to rely on their own headlamp to see. One unfortunate spelunker broke his light and had a difficult time navigating the cave as he tried to share his light with a fellow caver.

The men's legs were either soaked from crossing the river numerous times or mud-ridden from trying to stay dry and avoid the water. The weather and the events leading up to this caving activity had put the men in a bad mood. Spirits then moved to an all-time low when the temperature in the cave dropped dramatically.

Before exiting the long cave the men gathered in a large cavernous room. As they turned off their lights darkness engulfed every square inch. Bodies were cold and the darkness had quieted the soul. All of a sudden one of the men began to sing a familiar old hymn. The rest of the men joined in. The cave echoed with praise and worship lifting our voices to our heavenly Father.

It was too cold to execute the cave swim, so the men exited out on dry land and were greeted by the sun, which hadn't been seen all week. Cold and tired bodies exited the cave. Stepping into the warmth of the light was definitely worth the reward.

"Hope is like the sun, which, as we journey toward it, casts the shadow of our burden behind us." – Samuel Smiles

This trip was more challenging then it was relaxing. Cold and rainy weather, whitewater rafting, G.P.S. hiking, cave exploring, and outdoor camping during the first week of May, all made for tough conditions. Even with cold, dark and wet conditions inside the cave the men were still able to praise and worship our heavenly Father. Trials and tribulations are a part of life and often don't make any sense to us, but God understands and He will still receive honor and glory, even when we don't understand.

The struggle is worth the reward.

Read 2 Timothy 4, and then find a quiet place of solitude and sing your favorite hymn or praise and worship song to your heavenly Father.

"Now the serpent was more crafty than any other beast of the field that the Lord God had made. He said to the woman, "Did God actually say, 'You shall not eat of any tree in the garden'?" Genesis 3:1 (ESV)

THROUGH THE DARKNESS – PART 3

The cave swim was one of two ways to leave the cave. When the orders came from the lead guide and a former U.S. Army Ranger, that the cave swim was being cancelled mixed emotions emerged from the group of amateur spelunkers. Some of the men were relieved by the decision to call it off and others were greatly disappointed. Up to this point it had already been a cold and tiring adventure. Current sleeping conditions, outside air temperature and the frigid water all combined to build a case of not exposing the men to hypothermia.

A small group of men talked it over and decided they were going to do the cave swim, regardless of the order. Fortunately, no one was hurt, but it took some of the men quite a while before their core body temperature began to rise, warming them once again. There were some heated and lengthy discussions about why the orders were given and why the men should not have disobeyed those orders. It was explained that they put the leaders and the other hikers in a bad position if something bad had happened. After all, emergency help was not right around the corner. The men apologized and all was well after that.

"I gave in, and admitted that God was God" – C.S. Lewis

When you read the story of Adam and Eve you relive the first time man tried to become like God. This story is the beginning and the catalyst for the rest of humanity making an attempt to seek out "God Status". The Old Testament is filled with stories of men seeking ultimate power. For example, Cain took on the role of determining who gets to live and who dies, Lamech chose to change the rules of marriage, Nimrod and others sought to be as powerful as a god.

Lest we forget Satan's fall from heaven resulted from his rebellious attempt to sit in God's rightful place. As a result, the world mirrors his actions, because it is being influenced by the original author of rebellion, an angel, who is a liar, a thief and a murderer.

How many times do we try to set up our own rules, create our own timelines, and make demands for how our life is supposed to play out? Do we try to take matters into our own hands? Do we try to become men or women of power? Do we dictate to God (like Cain) what is an acceptable sacrifice?

In what ways do we try to take the place of God?

Read Genesis 3 and 4. Reflect on the actions of those seeking selfish gain.

"Blessed is the man who remains steadfast under trial, for when he has stood the test he will receive the crown of life, which God has promised to those who love him."
James 1:12 (ESV)

A CRAZY DAY

Have you ever had one of those mornings where the best laid plans fall apart? It all began for me when my wife left me in charge of our five children to go on a ladies' retreat. My only responsibilities were to let the dog out, feed the children, and make sure they all got to school on time. My wife is a planner and everything was arranged ahead of time so implementing her plan should've been fairly simple.

Unfortunately, a forgetful car pool driver, a child wetting the bed, a new puppy leaving gifts around the house, a child leaving her backpack behind, a car running on fumes, careless driving in front of a police officer, and two crazy phone calls that had all the drama of a daytime soap made for a chaotic first morning. The lone bright spot was not getting pulled over when I definitely deserved a ticket.

"Life is simple, it's just not easy." – Author Unknown

Our days are filled with responsibilities, activities, obstacles, trials and many other kinds of inconveniences. But they are all a part of life. Our spiritual lives work much in the same way. If we are seeking after God, we can expect that the evil one will not let us be free from trouble, temptation, and even persecution in some situations.

Satan is subtle and when you think your day is going great, he will find a way to wreck it. When you've just come off of a spiritual high, he will find a way to disqualify it. When you've been spiritually disciplined in an area of your life, he will work on a different area. When you're on your way to church, he will find a way to get you to fight. And when you finally answer God's call on your life, he will throw some darts at you to discourage and to distract.

But be encouraged and hang in there; nothing strange is happening to you, other than life itself and a little spiritual warfare. Lean heavily on God during these times and let His protection, peace and rest lay upon you.

What do you do when life gets crazy?

Think about your craziest of days and create a list concerning all that went wrong and then make a list about all that went right, or write concerning how it could've been worse. Read James 1.

"The fear of the Lord leads to life, and whoever has it rests satisfied; he will not be visited by harm." Proverbs 19:23 (ESV)

A FEAR OF GOD

The day was filled with hope and imagination until the dark storm clouds rolled in unannounced. The neighborhood gang comprised of playful children began to scatter in multiple directions as the first peals of thunder began booming across the open field. Victory would have to wait another day in our now rain-delayed game of summer backyard baseball.

With every flash of lightning the legs of one particular baseball player would leap and leave the ground in a desperate attempt to outrun the storm and avoid electrocution. The theory not based on any scientific fact, but just sheer childhood common sense which said, "Objects floating in mid-air cannot be struck by lightning."

"For as high as the heavens are above the earth, so great is his steadfast love toward those who fear him." – Psalm 103:11 ESV

Many times the fear response in a child is not based on reality, but instead out of some misguided idea floating around in their heads. As a child, I sought to be a good person because I didn't want to be target practice for a God who loved to zap little boys with lightning if they did something wrong. I definitely had a fear of God, but was it a healthy fear?

A proper fear of God is respecting Him for who He is. He is the creator of all life. He is your Guide and Shepherd. He is a God of love, compassion, mercy and gentleness, but you should never forget that He is also a God of holiness, righteousness, truth and justice. A healthy fear of God should direct your life to make choices that lead towards Him and not down a path of destruction.

Do you have a healthy fear of God?

Read Psalm 103, pray and write down at least 5 attributes of God from this chapter.

"And all the country of Judea and all Jerusalem were going out to him and were being baptized by him in the river Jordan, confessing their sins." Mark 1:5 (ESV)

IMPROPER BALANCE

The air and water temperature weren't favorable for a river tube float, but nothing was going to stop this group of men from completing the final event of their weekend adventure. Dressed more like winter ski bums than summer water sport enthusiasts, the men entered the river with care, displaying their own style and technique for boarding their tubes.

One of the men jump on his tube which immediately flipped over with him disappearing into the water. When he emerged another man, much bigger than he, blurted out, "What are you, an idiot?" The larger man proceeded to sit on his tube in an unorthodox manner, and you can guess what happened next. Ker-splash!! In his quest to prove that he could master the river tube he attempted the same move two more times with the same humiliating results. He was a great sport and provided a lasting memory for all involved.

"Sensuality is easily the biggest obstacle to godliness among men today and is wreaking havoc in the Church." – R. Kent Hughes

Was his problem positioning, balance, inexperience or an unorthodox entry?

Our sin nature often leaves us in a wrong position, off balance or entering into a humiliating or embarrassing sin. Like a splash in the river, it can be painful to endure the aftermath from the fallout from these sins. In addition, it can be a heavy burden debating with God the need to confess your sin.

Christ will help us remove the shame, guilt, humiliation and do away with all of the embarrassment of our sins. The Lord will uphold us as He is seated at the right hand of God. We are his children. He loves us and it is his desire to pull us up, not to sink us deeper. If we are struggling with sin it is important to know that Jesus Christ is there to help. If we truly seek repentance of our sins, He will immerse us in his forgiveness.

Confess to God first, and then confess to others.

Read John 8:1-11 and ask God for his help to overcome sin in your life. Are you a Christian? Have you been baptized?

SEIZE THE ADVENTURE – Commit with Passion

"There arose a great storm on the sea, so that the boat was being swamped by the waves; but he was asleep. And they went and woke him saying, "Save us, Lord; we are perishing." And he said to them, "Why are you afraid, O you of little faith?" Matthew 8:23-26 (ESV)

STORM ON THE WATER

The dark clouds rolled in bringing with them a sense of doom. It was summer and the fishing had been exceptional on this particular day. My father, an avid fisherman would spend all day fishing on this giant, northern Michigan pond. We were at least a half-hour from shore, so getting to safety wasn't even a possibility.

The threatening clouds broke open and launched a severe summer thunderstorm. Lightning bolts flew everywhere and the wind picked up, causing us to rock back and forth in the waves. Shore was far away; we would have to ride out the storm in a small metal row boat. I was scared to death.

"Then he rose and rebuked the winds and the sea, and there was a great calm. And the men marveled, saying, "What sort of man is this, that even winds and sea obey him?"

Storms are a regular part of life. They are inevitable, unavoidable, and most of the time they come out of nowhere. You may not be able to run from them, or even hide from them. But isn't it comforting to know that Christ is with you and he has the power to calm the rough waters of your life and to be with you even when things do not seem calm?

Not only does Jesus have power over creation, but he has the power over death, which makes Him almighty. If God is who we believe Him to be then there should be no reason to doubt that He is present in all of our situations. Be encouraged, He is in control and He will bring about a great calm in your life, if you let him in.

What area in your life do you need Christ's power to calm?

Read Matthew 8, pray and meditate on all of the miracles Jesus performed in this chapter.

"Judge not, that you be not judged. For with the judgment you pronounce you will be judged, and with the measure you use it will be measured to you." Matthew 7:1-2 (ESV)

NOT WHAT IT APPEARS

I love to travel to different states and see the creative variety of God's creation. I especially love many of the western states, such as Wyoming. A particular ranch located in that beautiful state is a place we have hunted in the past, and it is especially notable for a protruding mountainous red wall that runs through the ranch's land and beyond.

The ranch's red wall is a historical point of interest. It's where Butch Cassidy and his famous gang of smugglers became notorious for stealing cattle and disappearing without a trace. It was the perfect escape route and it always left the sheriff and his posse bewildered. Upon visiting this sight in person, you quickly come to the realization that it would be impossible to smuggle hundreds of cattle over the wall. But, when you explore and investigate the exact spot close up, you discover a switchback trail, hidden to the naked eye. Things aren't always what they appear.

"Why do you see the speck that is in your brother's eye, but do not notice the log that is in your own eye." – Jesus Christ

Situations and issues that arise in the lives of others or even in our own church may not always be what they appear. We need to keep this in mind when we make ill-informed decisions about how others should act or react in particular circumstances.

Do you know all of the facts? Do you know the reasons why someone chose to do something that goes against what you believe to be the smartest decision? Be careful not to judge a situation, especially when you may not know all of the information. In every situation, remain in the light and be a person of integrity, and try offering a loving and helping hand rather than offering a judgmental look or statement.

Do you spend more time looking at others or yourself?

If you have inappropriately judged a situation, go to that person and seek forgiveness.

"When I look at your heavens, the work of your fingers, the moon and the stars, which you have set in place, what is man that you are mindful of him, and the son of man that you care for him?"
Psalm 8:3-4 (ESV)

WHY A NERD WOULD HIKE – Jerry Foster

A friend of mine, Jerry Foster, wrote this after participating in a Grand Canyon adventure with me to Havasu Falls, a place filled with dust, desert and a large canyon. But we shouldn't forget about the lush green foliage surrounding the crystal clear water running over three major waterfalls. It is a sight to see, including the night-time view of the sky that holds more stars than the grains of sand on a beach.

My back hurt. So did my shoulders. I was freezing and felt like I'm in a fog. My mind tries to focus, to give me some clues to why I was laying there in pain, in the dark. Then reality arrived ever so slowly. I was in a tent in the middle of nowhere, as in, if-I-cut-my-finger-I-bleed-to-death middle of nowhere. Why was I doing this again?

I enjoy being indoors, especially in my office. What's not to love? Seventy-six degrees, comfortable chair, sterile desk, and wonderful artificial light provided by halogen lamps and computer screens. Snacks, books, games, TV, and the internet are all within arm's reach. But what are you to do when you realize that your skin is just a bit too much this side of pasty white? What should you do when you grow tired of the media onslaught? And what is a good response when you start to wonder if spiritual life is getting stale?

Perhaps a trip outdoors is the answer. You know, that big, wide-open, scary place with bugs, humidity, and yes, dirt. A few years ago I hiked with a group down to the bottom of the Grand Canyon and camped for four days by the stunning Havasu Falls. And more recently I embarked on a northern Michigan kayak adventure.

"The heavens declare the glory of God, and the sky above proclaims his handiwork."

Each trip was a fantastic encounter, bonding with other guys, pushing my M&M-starved body physically, laughing until I nearly cried, and most of all, reconnecting with the God who made me and loves me. It was amazing to me just how easy it is to live every day in the midst of God's awesome creation yet consistently take it for granted by not taking the time to fully appreciate and absorb it. Not until you've sat on a hill in the middle of nowhere with absolutely no light pollution to dilute the sight of millions of stars on a pitch black night does the impact of what the Psalmist is saying really hit home.

Do you take God's creation for granted?

Spend a weekend of solitude in the wilderness connecting with God in His creation.

"To do righteousness and justice is more acceptable to the Lord than sacrifice."
Proverbs 21:3 (ESV)

NOT ALWAYS GO BIG OR GO HOME

A small buck slowly approached my shooting lane. I wasn't interested. My sights were set on shooting a trophy whitetail. The deer eventually passed out of sight, but it wouldn't be until later that I would regret that decision. I told myself that it was for quality game management purposes, but really it was more about going big.

Later in the season, during the rut, a large trophy eight point sauntered into view. Desperate to shoot another deer worth hanging on the wall, I was impatient and rushed my shot. Misjudging the yardage, my arrow fell well short of my intended target. I would not see another deer the rest of the season and in hindsight, I should not have passed on the previous deer to go for the trophy that was outside of my reach.

"The Bible tells us to love our neighbors, and also to love our enemies; probably because they are generally the same people." – G.K. Chesterton

God is always working in our lives. I'm learning that he doesn't always want me to go big when he has some small things for me to do first. I am all for stepping out in faith and seeking to do great things for God, and we should. But, remember that God doesn't always need us or ask us to do the impossible.

Sometimes he just wants us to be content where we are and do what comes natural. Talking to a neighbor or helping them out during a time of need. Serving in nursery at church or engaging in some other low profile ministry opportunity. Keeping a journal helps us praise Him for all he has done for us, but also, so that we can see how he works in each of us in both big ways and through our small deeds.

Are there any small things that you could do for God?

Read Ruth 1-2 and take note of the faithfulness and sacrifice of Ruth and Boaz.

 "For everything there is a season, and a time for every matter under heaven." Ecclesiastes 3:1 (ESV)

GRACE LIKE RAIN

If all went well, the tube float would last about two hours. Laughing and splashing could be heard within earshot, up and down the river, as ladies climbed on their tubes and began a relaxing float on the cool waters of the Au' Sable river in northern Michigan. Conditions were perfect this beautiful summer day.

However, the unexpected would come quickly; only fifteen minutes into the trip a thunderstorm rolled in fast and caught us all by surprise. The air temperature dropped what felt like twenty degrees and the ensuing hour long downpour-chilled everyone to the bone. The participants were helpless and had to wait for the current of the river to eventually bring them to their final destination.

"Your worst days are never so bad that you are beyond the reach of God's grace. And your best days are never so good that you are beyond the need of God's grace." – Jerry Bridges

Another time we were whitewater rafting with a group of teens on the New River in West Virginia when an extremely intense thunderstorm overtook us half way through our whitewater adventure. The storm became an even bigger threat when lightning bolt after lightning bolt lit up the canyon. The roar of thunder echoed in the canyon, drowning out any sound of the raging river.

Even the guides were afraid. Where do we take cover? We had a dilemma on our hands: should we pull off the river and hide under trees being targeted by lightning or do we stay exposed in the middle of the river?

Life is filled with unexpected situations. Sometimes it pours and other times it seems like everything comes crashing down on us. The circumstances we find ourselves in usually come as a surprise, but regardless, getting through them safely all depends on the grace and strength of God. Be content, be safe, and draw near to Christ in times of trouble.

Expect the unexpected.

Let God's grace rain down?

Read Ecclesiastes 3:1-8 and spend time in prayer reflecting on God's grace in your life.

> "God opposes the proud, but gives grace to the humble. Submit yourselves therefore to God. Resist the devil and he will flee from you. Draw near to God and he will draw near to you." James 4:7-8a (ESV)

UNDERCURRENT WARNING

We had travelled over eight hours to whitewater raft on the New River in West Virginia. Rain in the area was causing the river to reach its maximum height allowed for recreational rafting. The outfitter was contemplating closing down, but decided that since we were still within a few inches of the danger level that we could continue with our trip as planned.

The lead instructor warned us that due to the fast water that it would not be smart to leave the boat at any time during the trip. Half-way through our adventure we hit a section of river that was calm and without rapids. Without warning the guide in our boat ran from the back of the raft and sprang off the rubber bow, performing a flip before diving into the water and disappearing. The laughter from the other guides gave way to looks of concern and worry when their colleague didn't resurface in a timely fashion.

The guide eventually popped up downstream, but not after a long struggle with the undercurrents of this powerful river. He was eventually pulled to safety and returned to our boat. The look on his face told us that this had been no practical joke. The guide had not heeded the warning of the lead instructor, needlessly putting himself in danger.

> *"Many of us suffer from temptations from which we have no business to suffer."*
> *— Oswald Chambers*

This world is filled with an undercurrent of sin and temptation that can entangle even the best of us. Sometimes the consequences of our choices can't be seen on the surface, but once you go deeper is the real danger made clear. The evil one is subtle, he is the author of lies, and it his quest to seek your destruction.

Is there an undercurrent of sin present in your life?

Read James 4 and pray that God would help you identify potential problem areas in your life. Take some time to think about how you can develop strategies to overcome them.

"Walk by the Spirit, and you will not gratify the desires of the flesh." Galatians 5:16 (ESV)

SCOPE ADJUSTMENT

The dusty canyon was rocky, winding, and narrow. It was an ideal place to stalk a bedded-down trophy mule deer buck. Stalking quietly, I made my way up the canyon. A slight breeze blowing into my face let me know my approach would go undetected. My boots, clothing, and rifle were covered in orange dust. Gripping the rifle, ready for anything, I pressed on.

Out of nowhere, a prized 5 x 5 mule deer leapt from his hidden resting place and took off running. His route would allow me to take a couple of shots at him as he ran away. I popped the rifle to my shoulder and pressed the 9x power scope to my eye. I could see nothing but fur filling up the lens of my scope.

I learned a valuable lesson that day. Never hunt with your rifle scope on full power until you have your target in your sights and then you can zero in on them much better. When the scope is on 9x the deer fills up the entire scope, so when the deer is running it is hard to locate it. I should have set my scope at a 2x or 3x, or dropped down and used my iron sights, especially with a running deer. If I had done this properly, I may have had great success.

"The desires of the flesh are temporary, but the Spirit is eternal."

Set your sights on developing a deeper relationship with Jesus Christ. Do you have the right focus? Are you focusing in on the Spirit or in the flesh?

Reading the Scriptures and praying can sometimes seem cliché, but if you want to stay dialed in to God's will for your life, you won't neglect the tools needed to keep the faith. When the desires of the flesh fill up your sight, you will miss the mark. But when your scope is dialed in to the Spirit, you will hit the mark.

Do you have God completely in your sights?

Read Galatians 5:16-26 and find a place of solitude to take a few minutes to pray to God.

"But God chose what is foolish in the world to shame the wise; God chose what is weak in the world to shame the strong" 1 Corinthians 1:27 (ESV)

A REJECTED PLAYER

The feel of summer had left the air and in its place the smell of fall wafted across the players' noses. It was football season, time to put the pads on once again and hit somebody, in Christian love, of course. The coaches barked out orders and blew their whistles and the players did their best to snap at every command.

The coaches grabbed kids by their face masks and pulled them to areas marked by position. Ken was placed in the offensive line circle, designated as a center. It was the beginning of the practice season and positions were already being decided. The coaches looked at Ken's build and said he couldn't play the high profile positions, like running back, quarterback or wide-receiver. The coaches rejected Ken for various reasons without ever giving him a chance.

Late in the season and after numerous played games, the defensive coach decided to scrimmage his starting defense against a group of non-skilled players, like the offensive line and guys who sat the bench. It was his desire to boost his defense's confidence by letting them pulverize this rag-tag offensive group. Ken, the center, along with his slender 6' 3" frame was chosen as a wide receiver. He was fast and shined in this position, making miracle catch after miracle catch. The coaches were stunned and Ken finished out the season as the team's starting wide-receiver.

> *"Prayer girds human weakness with divine strength, turns human folly into heavenly wisdom, and gives troubled mortals the peace of God. We know not what prayer can do." – C. Spurgeon*

Like the coaches rejecting Ken without ever giving him a shot, I too had influential people in my life tell me that I would never be a leader, a public speaker or a writer. In fact, in high school those three disciplines were probably my three weakest. Now as an adult I work at all three of those things. God likes to use the weakness of man to do great works for Him and when He moves in us, we cannot boast about our own strength, but must give God the honor and glory.

Even if man rejects you, God won't.

What is your biggest weakness that God can use for His glory?

Read 1 Peter 2 and write down one spiritual/ministry thing that you have no business trying and then pray and ask God to work to use you in that way. It may be preaching, teaching, mission trip, or other.

SEIZE THE ADVENTURE – Commit with Passion

"Consider Him who endured from sinners such hostility against himself, so that you may not grow weary or fainthearted. In your struggle against sin you have not yet resisted to the point of shedding your blood."
Hebrews 12:3-4 (ESV)

GET OUT OF THE FOG

It was early in the morning and the all-day men's softball tournament had just begun. A white softball the same color as the clouds was lobbed overhead and flew through the air before disappearing into a grey, dense fog. It rolled to the fence and the batter was easily able to score an inside the park home-run. Our team was down many runs in the first inning before we learned that our outfielders couldn't see the ball when it was hit. The tournament officials couldn't afford to postpone any of the games, so we had to play no matter what. It was the end of the first inning before the infield learned to yell to our outfielders which direction the ball was travelling.

We lost our first game of the tourney, which meant we had to play the rest of our games in the "loser's" bracket. Our team fought all the way through the "loser's" bracket and eventually found ourselves sitting in the championship game facing the best team who was undefeated. In the final inning we scored a run to both win the game and force a second championship game, as both teams had one loss each. The second game, a hard fought battle, came down to the final out to determine the winner. An inside the park home-run would secure the victory for our team. We spent the rest of the following week recovering from the soreness and pain of playing so many games. In the end it was all worth it to come home with the trophy.

> *"Faith is like radar that sees through the fog-the reality of things at a distance that the human eye cannot see." – Corrie Ten Boom*

We were able to pull it together and win the entire tournament. It wasn't easy and it definitely took time to accomplish our goal. Whatever trials or tribulations you are currently facing may be daunting to you, but it is not to God. Lean on Him and trust in Him. It may take some time and involve some pain but eventually you will have victory over your problems. Keep working hard and moving forward inning by inning.

It is never too late to get out of a fog and win it all!

Talk with God about confessing past sins and asking for the grace, peace and strength to move forward from your darkness and have spiritual victory.

"Therefore I tell you, do not be anxious about your life, what you will eat or what you will drink, nor about your body, what you will put on. Is not life more than food and the body more than clothing?"
Matthew 6:25 (ESV)

ALL OF THE TOYS

Too many times when we get involved in an outdoor activity we feel the need to have the latest accessories, clothing or top-notch equipment. Somehow we convince ourselves that we must have these items in order to be successful. I have fished using hotdogs for bait and I've been fishing with a professional guide and all of the "best" bait and equipment. I have shot deer while wearing jeans and a t-shirt and also while wearing "professional" gear, but which times were the most rewarding?

"Toys are nice, but you can't take them with you."

Hunting, fishing, and outdoor activities are not meant to be about the latest gear or the fancy clothing. It is not about getting the biggest trophy, or having the best story. It is supposed to be about the experience, the chase, or the time spent with your sporting partners, friends and family.

God wants our daily lives to be about the heart and the experience that we can have with Him. Life was not intended to be about the earthly fads that quickly die away, but a life filled with eternal perspective. God wants us to put our faith and trust in Him. He takes care of the birds and the flowers, how much more does He care about us? He will provide, protect and sustain us. He knows that LIFE is more than the things of this world; He just wants us to realize it too. Be smart with your money, your time, and life focus, and your God and your family will love you for it.

What is consuming your time and energy toys, or people?

Read Matthew 6 to see what life is really about.

SEIZE THE ADVENTURE – Commit with Passion

"His invisible attributes, namely, his eternal power and divine nature, have been clearly perceived, ever since the creation of the world, in the things that have been made. So they are without excuse."
Romans 1:20 (ESV)

A SPECIAL REVERENCE AND AWE

The seemingly endless beach and superfluity of water in Lake Michigan was an awe inspiring view. The curvature of the earth could be seen off in the distance, displaying a beautiful sunset filled with various hues of orange, red, purple, and blue. The sun began its slow descent behind the horizon, setting the stage for that moment of silence which follows the minute or two it takes for it to disappear for the evening.

Experiencing a scene like this mandates hushed reverence followed by a smattering of quiet praise. Any observer who wants to can experience a masterpiece like this physically, audibly, visually, and emotionally. For example, a refreshing breeze gently wrapping around a person and then quietly disappearing, only to return from where it came, influences you physically. The comforting sound of the waves gently lapping onto the shore and the occasional squeak from a passing seagull, affects people audibly. Viewing the multiple shades of colors that coat the sky and then fill the lake with water, impacts everyone visually. The privilege of standing on the pure, sandy beach during a moment like this will undoubtedly have an emotional effect on our hearts and minds.

> *"A master of art, God paints the sky, pulling it all into one enormous living portrait. An artist who can weave this kind of artistry, creativity and intelligence into a natural canvas of this magnitude is more than an artist, He is a Supernatural Designer."* – Michael Tison

The author of life, God, has created one gigantic universe and even worlds within worlds that seem to cohabitate and complement each other. It is an amazing complexity and interweaving of intricate detail into each of these worlds, such as space, galaxies, planets, stars, moons, suns, a world of animals, fish, birds, bugs, ecosystems, microscopic creatures, mountains, oceans, lakes, rivers, deserts and last but definitely not least the amazing human body. Is this an artist's creation worthy of our attention?

If God were to examine your life would it hold up to scrutiny and demonstrate a walk filled with reverence and awe?

Read Romans 1:18-25 and take a few minutes to honor God with reverence and awe.

 "The Lord will rescue me from every evil deed and bring me safely into his heavenly kingdom. To him be the glory forever and ever. Amen." 2 Timothy 4:18 (ESV)

CRAZY CREATION

On a family vacation to the Smokey Mountains in Tennessee we visited the town of Gatlinburg, "The Gateway to the Smokey Mountains." During the day we spent the hours hiking and investigating the beautiful national park. But at night, my wife and I and our five children went into town in search of something new. We were looking for a combination of value and quality and since most of our options were tourist traps, our choices were limited.

Finally, we decided that our best value was visiting Ripley's Aquarium. Wow! What a great choice and a wonderful time we had looking at all of the amazing creatures. It was pretty obvious looking at all of these deadly sea and land creatures that God, not evolution, had created these awesome, living things. We saw black and neon poisonous dart frogs, killer jellyfish, deadly stingrays, man-eating sharks, and a ton of cute little fish that would bite your head off if you looked the other way. Most of the sea creatures here eliminated any reason to attempt catch and release.

"Men do not differ much about what things they will call evils; they differ enormously about what evils they will call excusable." – G.K. Chesterton

Our world is filled with danger. Some of it is obvious, but many of the perils we face are wrapped in beauty, disguising their real intent. For example, the Blue-Ringed Octopus has brilliant blue rings that glow when angry and uses these mesmerizing rings to warn others to be aware. This particular species is the most deadly of all octopuses. It produces toxic and lethal venom strong enough to kill humans.

The evil one always wraps sin up in a beautiful container, but when you open it poison leaks out. An adulterous woman is beautiful to the eye, but lethal poison to one's spiritual life. Our spiritual lives are always open to attack by the evil one. Be alert! Be prepared! Stand firm in your faith and know that you have a King who will protect you from the evil that lurks around you. There will be warning signs, you just have to look and be prepared by reading your Bible and praying without ceasing.

Are you still unsure?

Seek out a man who has great discernment and ask him for spiritual advice.

Read 2 Timothy 2 and memorize key verses that will help you build up a defense for spiritual protection.

SEIZE THE ADVENTURE – Commit with Passion

"For this reason I remind you to fan into flame the gift of God, which is in you through the laying on of my hands, for God gave us a spirit not of fear but of power and love and self-control." 2 Timothy 1:6-7 (ESV)

FAN THE FLAME

The day was overcast and extremely windy; everything had dried up. Spring fever hit and three boys needed to get out of their houses. Their rally point was across the field and many acres from the nearest home.

One of the boys had a lighter and began to ignite small patches of weeds and then would quickly stomp out the mini-fires he'd started. He passed the lighter to the next boy who followed suit. A big gust of wind fanned a small fire into a medium –sized flame which continued to grow at a rapid rate. All of the boys began to stomp on that fire, throw dirt on it in an attempt to extinguish the growing flames. Realizing the fire was out-of-control, two of the boys told the other one to stay and fight the fire while they ran to get help.

Running down the trail while formulating a plan to get out of the mess, we turned back to see our lone fire-fighter running right behind us with a giant flame chasing him down. Twenty-foot flames licked at our heels as the gusty wind continued to feed this growing monster. We made it to the house and called the fire department. My father quickly realized that his watering hose would be no match for this raging inferno. The fire department arrived and spent hours putting out the fire. It had spread quickly and burned many acres of open field near our home. It was travelling on its way to an inaccessible area which could have burned down hundreds of acres of forest and swamp.

> *"Give me the love that leads the way, The faith that nothing can dismay, The hope no disappointments tire, The passion that will burn like fire, Let me not sink to be a clod: Make me Thy fuel, Flame of God." – Amy Carmichael*

We learned that day the awesome power of mixing wind and fire to devastating effect. Ever since, I have developed a healthy and deep respect of the danger of playing with fire. However, there is one time and place to mix those two elements and that is in our spiritual lives. When we start a fire in our hearts by seeking after God, reading the Bible, praying and engaging in total surrender the Holy Spirit will come along and fan that spark into a raging flame, if we choose to walk in the Spirit.

Have you lost that spark?

What will it take to get it back?

Read 2 Timothy 1 and meditate on what it will take to get that spark back in your Christian walk. If you've never lost it what can you do to fan that flame into a larger fire?

"Let not your hearts be troubled. Believe in God; believe also in me. In my Father's house are many rooms. If it were not so, would I have told you that I go to prepare a place for you?"
John 14:1-2 (ESV)

GOING HOME

Twilight was coming to a close. Darkness filled the air and the evening's final deer slowly moved out of sight. Our adventure and hunt had come to an end. Our final preparations for the evening began as we holstered our arrows, unbuckled our safety belts, and carefully lowered our bows to the earth. The ladder stands creaked underneath our weight as we descended to the forest floor.

My pre-teen son and I talked for a few minutes about the day's hunt and then began our short hike home. Remnants of the sunset still lingered around the edges of the gathering clouds. The leaves crunched noisily as we trekked through the woods. I began to thank our God and our heavenly Father for such a beautiful day, and then as we approached the edge of the woods the warm and glowing lights of our house welcomed us. This brought additional praise and thanks, for a loving family and the blessings of a warm home.

"We talk about heaven being so far away. It is within speaking distance to those who belong there." – Dwight L. Moody

Looking at our house reminded me of my boyhood home. My mother passed away at the relatively young age of 63. While on earth, it was her intent to provide us with a warm and welcoming home. As all mothers go, she provided for our family and did her best to meet all of our fickle needs. She was a great woman, but most importantly, a godly woman.

Although she has preceded us in death, it warms my heart knowing that Jesus Christ was with her as she walked through the darkness and towards the warm and welcoming Light of heaven. Our time here on earth is temporary and our life focus should not be on staying home, but rather going home to a place of eternal rest.

Are you ready for home?

Read Revelation 21 and 22 and take the rest of your life to dwell on the things above.

Faith Challenge Adventure

If you are looking for an activity to awaken your faith, try participating in what I call the Faith Challenge Adventure. The scriptural basis for this idea comes from Luke 10 when Jesus sends out the "72" to prepare the way for His ministry. In the same way, you and another person will go out and engage in ministry.

Here is how this easy challenge works:

1. Pray about partnering up with a person who is looking to awaken their faith and who is willing to be a part of your two-person adventure team. This person must be committed and willing to step out on faith. Are you?

2. Meet with this person, read Luke 10 and discuss how God might use the two of you to do great things for His ministry. It could be:
    a. A missions trip or service adventure to another state or country
    b. Being part of an evangelism or outreach event
    c. Helping out a local ministry (ex. Soup kitchen, crisis pregnancy center, etc...)
    d. A week of wilderness solitude praising and worshipping God
    e. Financially supporting another ministry
    f. Or some other activity that involved love, service or sacrifice

3. Pray about this for a few weeks and then gather a second time and discuss what God has been speaking to your hearts.

4. Make a plan, set a time table, and pray that God would provide the funds and other resources needed to pull off this faith challenge adventure. Pray some more.

5. Participate in the activity that was chosen and see God work.

6. Report the details of your story back to the author at mtison@seizetheadventure.com with a picture and a written account of how God moved during your Faith Challenge experience.

ABOUT THE AUTHOR

Mike Tison speaks to men, outdoor enthusiasts, and churches across the country. He holds a master's degree in Theological Studies from Liberty University. He loves hunting and the outdoors, and founded His2Overcome Adventure Ministries (H2O) to encourage people to view God, His creation, and their lives with passion and enthusiasm. An ordained pastor, Mike lives in Michigan with his wife, Sarah, and their five children.

To contact Mike or to book him for your next special event go to:

www.SeizeTheAdventure.com

ACKNOWLEDGMENTS

Thank you to my beautiful wife, Sarah, the perfect helpmate and friend, for your sacrificial heart and for your love. To my children, Kayla, Zachary, Seth, Micah and Lydia: you bring great joy to my life and I am proud of each of you. Micah, I hope to read *your* published book one day soon.

A special thanks to Sandra Byrd for helping polish this endeavor and to Pat Stefanyk and Laura Tokie for helping find the best in my writing along the way. Thanks, too, to Kevin Shorkey and Hillside Bible Church for his support for my entire ministry endeavors. PK, you are the very reason this book has been written. I appreciate your encouragement and continuing challenge to step out of my comfort zone. Thank you to my favorite in-law parents for loving me as one of your own. And last but not least, a special thanks to my father, brother and sister for igniting a passion in me for outdoor activities and for putting me in position to tell many of these stories.

All praise, glory and honor are God's. Thank you, God for using weak men like me to accomplish YOUR plans.

Adventure Notes:

Adventure Notes:

Adventure Notes:

Adventure Notes:

Adventure Notes:

Adventure Notes:

Adventure Notes:

Adventure Notes:

SEIZE THE ADVENTURE – Commit with Passion

Prayer Journal:　　　　　　　　　　　**Yes　No　Grow**

Prayer Journal:　　　　　　　　　　　**Yes No Grow**

SEIZE THE ADVENTURE – Commit with Passion

Prayer Journal: **Yes No Grow**

Prayer Journal: **Yes No Grow**

SEIZE THE ADVENTURE – Commit with Passion

Prayer Journal: **Yes No Grow**

Prayer Journal: **Yes No Grow**

SEIZE THE ADVENTURE – Commit with Passion

Prayer Journal: **Yes No Grow**

Prayer Journal: **Yes No Grow**

_____
_____
_____
_____
_____
_____
_____
_____
_____
_____
_____
_____
_____
_____
_____
_____
_____
_____
_____
_____

Made in the USA
Charleston, SC
02 December 2012